Cheaper Than Therapy

Joy, healing
& life lessons in fiber

Compiled & Edited by
Annie Modesitt

Mode
Knit
Press

Copy Editor: Lissy Friedman

Text copyright ©2005 Annie Modesitt
*Each author retains full rights to each of their pieces, all inquiries pertaining
to republishing of any essay in this book should be directed to the author of
that specific piece.*

Printed in the USA by Fidlar/Doubleday
ISBN 0-9754219-8-0
ISBN 978-0-9754219-8-7 (13 digit)
2nd printing, 9/30/05 rev 1.
Cover Illustration: Annie Modesitt
Production: ModeKnit Press

Acknowledgments

First and foremost, I would like to thank the contributors of this book. Their essays moved me each time I read them, and I felt honored that they trusted their beautiful words to me.

I would like to thank my husband, Gerry Landy, who supports and sustains me as I fly from one hare brained scheme to another. I would thank my kids, but they're yelling at each other in the living room so they're off the list. *Sorry, kids, maybe next book...*

Thanks to Lissy Friedman for coming to my copy editing and proofing rescue. You make Strunk & White (and your mother) proud!

(Should that have been a comma?)

I would like to thank my blog readers who give me so much support and great advice (not to mention so many leads on wonderful essays!)

Thank you to each of my students — you teach me more than I could ever teach you!

Thanks to Jan, who always believes in me; and Karen, who always makes me laugh!

Most of all I'd like to thank family who have gone ahead. They are the genesis of this book, as it evolved from my own experience of grief, yarn, needles and fiber.

Thanks Mom!

Contents

Contents

Introduction

I'm lucky, I knit for a living. I never understood how fortunate I am until I began to experience a long run of bad luck. Oddly, each new, terrible, awesome thing which happened didn't push me into a funk, but somehow allowed me to see how truly blessed my life is. I think, in large part, this is the miracle of fiber.

Knitting keeps me sane, it keeps me busy, it keeps my mind calm and my heart full. I draw strength from the time I spend with my yarn, and — when I was unable to earn a living any other way — a world of designing, and writing opened up to me. I am very lucky.

During a period of mourning I began to write essays comparing finishing a sweater with finishing a life. I thought about publishing them on their own, but they seemed lonely. They wanted to be with other, similar essays. In speaking with my students as I taught across the country, I realized that many, many folks also shared my experience of grieving and finding peace through fiber.

This book represents the labor of so many talented folks who have submitted essays and edited these pieces. They express the joy, peace, fulfillment and comfort which a good ball of yarn can bring.

I hope you enjoy all that is reflected in each of these essays. I love them.

Annie Modesitt

Be good to yourself. If you are feeling at the end of your rope, hopeless, and things seem very dark, please seek the counsel of a good friend or a professional — you don't have to fight your demons alone.

Yarn does amazing things, it can change lives, but sometimes there is no substitute for therapy! Take care of yourself!

Cheaper Than Therapy

Joy, healing & life lessons in fiber

Monsters in the Merino

Gail Lucas

Yarn Shops used to be the most terrifying places on earth. They were full of nasty, vicious monsters, just waiting to pounce on anyone who wandered in. I'd rather have stayed home and knit with Red Heart Supersaver than get anywhere near a yarn shop.

See, there are days when I think I'm afraid of everything. Well, anything involving people. I'm terrified of being evaluated, of saying the wrong thing, of sounding like an idiot. I have *Social Anxiety Disorder*, also known as Social Phobia. Individuals with Social Anxiety Disorder experience intense, debilitating fear of social interactions, according to literature from the Madison Institute of Medicine.®†

Exactly what form Social Anxiety Disorder takes depends on the individual — some only have problems with public speaking, whereas others suffer from a range of fears including eating with others, meeting new people, dealing with authority figures, writing in front of others or using public bathrooms.

I have Generalized Social Anxiety, which means I suffer in a variety of situations. In particular, I am terrified of people I perceive to be in a position of authority. I also have a very hard time using the telephone, attending parties and meeting new people. I grew up as a shy child, but I was a fairly normal teenager. I had a few good friends, a boyfriend, and did well in school. However, by the time I finished college I was so filled with anxiety that I couldn't eat in the school cafeteria, and rarely left my room except to attend class and go to work. I didn't know that social anxiety existed — I grew up being told that everyone was shy, that everyone was scared of social interaction, but they found a way out of it. I felt that I was weak and a coward.

Despite my shyness, I graduated from college, attended graduate school (although I left after one year because I was too terrified to speak with my advisor, a leader in his field), and found a very good job in the computer industry. In some ways I'm lucky, I'm often able to fake my way through difficult social situations by acting a part. I worked as a telephone technical support representative for years by becoming *Tech Support Gail* — a woman who could distribute complex computer assistance freely on the phone, while the real me couldn't answer the phone at home at all.

My life was closing in around me. Despite having a boyfriend and a good job, I had no friends — I couldn't even make myself go to work-related social events and I could barely speak to my manager.

But I discovered a new hobby — knitting. I stumbled onto it accidentally, through an internet shopping experience. My great grandmother had taught me how to crochet when I was young, and noticing a deeply discounted afghan kit on a craft website, I bought it, assuming it was for crochet. I hadn't crocheted for years but heck — instructions were included — how difficult could it be?

I received the kit and was shocked when I realized it was a knitting project! I swear the instructions were in greek. I am stubborn, however, and I wanted to make an afghan. So, I went back to the same craft website, found a book called <u>Learn-to-Knit Afghan</u>, by Barbara Walker. *"Perfect!"* I thought, *"I want to knit an afghan, and here's a book that will show me how."* I ordered a bunch of Red Heart Super Saver acrylic, some needles, and learned to cast on.

To this day, I love that book. It is dog eared and falling apart, but knitting those 63 squares provided me with hours when I wasn't terrified, frightened, or lonely. For the first time in years, I could spend hours without my heart feeling as if it would pound its way out of my chest. I didn't care that the yarn was scratchy, and that the colors I picked didn't match — my stomach didn't hurt and I was happy! (The afghan eventually ended up as a series of dog and cat blankets — I realized I'd never use a beige and peach blanket that didn't even vaguely match.)

One day, while knitting one those squares on the Red Line on my way home from work, I saw an advertisement; participants with Social Anxiety Disorder were being sought for a research study. By this time, thanks to a television ad, I knew that Social Anxiety Disorder actually existed. Yes, it took one of those annoying pharmaceutical commercials to make me realize that not everyone almost threw up every time they had to say hello to their manager. While I knew it existed, I was too terrified to actually try to seek help.

But, I figured, if a massive sign was practically flashing over my head, perhaps someone meant for me to get better.

It took days, but I finally worked up the nerve to call the number. After going through the evaluation process, it was determined that I had a raging case of Social Anxiety Disorder — not as bad as some, given that I could keep a job — but still pretty bad. I started on medication, and my life opened up a tiny bit. I was a little more confident, I wasn't constantly terrified, but I still had one big issue.

Yarn shops — yes, yarn shops. I was terrified of them. Why? Because I was convinced that there was this vast body of knitting knowledge of which I knew nothing, and that everyone in the yarn shop would immediately know I was clueless. And judge me because of it. I've always been particularly intimidated by older women, and young folks weren't really knitting — the furry scarf craze hadn't started yet. But by this time I had finished my 63 squares and I wanted another project.

I knew that there was a yarn shop in my neighborhood, but the idea of actually walking in the door would make me burst into tears. I was petrified of being evaluated, of seeming stupid, of not knowing what to do. The first time I went I literally bolted to the back of the store, mumbled something inaudible to the clerk and grabbed the first magazine I saw.

I found a pretty pillow I wanted to knit, but I couldn't find the yarn it called for, or figure out how to substitute yarns. It didn't help that my heart was pounding so hard that I could barely think. I knew that the clerk was thinking I was the biggest idiot ever (not to mention the nasty monsters I was sure were hiding behind all the yarn.) I had to ask for help.

Finally, having bought yarn, a magazine and some needles, I fled. It took months before I worked up the nerve to return. But I kept at it — my desire to knit overcoming my terror. As I became more comfortable in yarn shops, I realized that I was becoming more comfortable in other situations, too. I began going to the after-work outings.

Knitting also helped me get through the research study — at the half way point, half of us were switched to a placebo. Lucky me, I managed to be in the placebo group, and my anxiety returned full force. It had never completely gone away, but it was now back so badly that I couldn't sleep. I sat on my couch, shaking, while I knitted and knitted, trying to hold on to the progress I had made. I forced myself go to yarn shops. I attended my first knitting convention, and even took classes. The classes were my first introduction to other knitters, and I realized that I was a better knitter than I thought. My classes were full of older women, but they were warm and welcoming.

My desire to knit helped me make progress with my social anxiety. Nothing else in my life could motivate me in the same way.

Four years later, I love going to yarn shops. I attend a regular knitting group, I have friends, my career is going great, and I even have a knitting blog which 100 people read each day.

Am I still scared? Sure. I'll always be shy and introverted, and I'll probably take medication for the rest of my life. I recently had to force myself to go into a bead shop for the first time. I call the shop *"The Scary Bead Store"*, which has caught on in my knitting group. But I wanted to make beaded stitch markers, so I made myself go — and I even asked for help.

Are there still scary yarn shop monsters drooling on the merino? Some days, yes. But most days I banish them with my needles rather than flee in terror.

†The Madison Institute of Medicine® is a non-profit institution providing educational booklets on mental health disorders.

Gail lives in Downers Grove, IL with her boyfriend, Kevin and her cat, Katie. When she's not knitting up a storm, you can find her actually making a living in the computer software industry, reading far too many books, and keeping up with her knitting blog, www.knittergail.com.

Knitting Yarn?

Regina Gonzalez

Maybe I am old school, or have just been hiding under a rock for the last decade, but when did yarn go beyond its mere yarn state and become Knitting Yarn?

I thought that all yarn was fair game when considering a needlework project. And when did all of these self-avowed knitters become unionized anyway? Read the first couple of sentences Amazon.com uses to pitch Debbie Stoller's book Stitch'n Bitch Nation:

> *Join the movement! Millions strong and counting, hip, young chicks with sticks are putting a whole new spin on knitting — while turning Stitch 'N Bitch: The Knitter's Handbook into a surprise bestseller*
>
> — *The New York Times*

I don't know about anyone else, but I've been knitting, crocheting, sewing, weaving and needlepointing since I was seven — that's 29 years. Okay, I didn't learn how to weave on a loom until college, but you get the point.

When my grandmother, of Eastern European ancestry, taught me how to do all of these things, she didn't tell me that crocheting was not as hip as knitting, and both take a backseat to sewing — or at least they did a decade ago. Not at all. Furthermore, when we went to our LYS (Local Yarn Shop — another term with which I've recently become familiar) we were not confronted by leagues of young, hip knitters donning Isadora

Duncan length scarves knit from eyelash yarn on gi-normous plastic needles.

No, we went to our local Super Yarn Mart, a staple in the Los Angeles area, whose shelves were filled with [gasp] acrylic yarn and whose aisles were heavily traveled by the blue-haired contingent. I loved it there. I loved that I was a little kid in a grown-up world who was able to knit a mean sweater in hours — intarsia, even — and that I could make enough granny squares to fill the bed of a Dodge Ram truck. *Oh yeah!*

I was good and I was hanging out with my Nana, whom I adored. What could be better than that?

No, we were never confronted by the Nouveau Knitter, wearing a scarf knitted with several $46, 50-yard hanks of fiber (you just cannot call 50 yards of anything costing $46 just plain yarn.) No, we were greeted by other blue-hairs working the register in between cig breaks. Aaaaaah, those were the good ol' days!

Okay, now don't get me wrong. I love that all of these "women's" crafts have become popular — I think it's great! However, what I do find strange is the fact that knitting is supposedly more highbrow than any other type of needlework.

This, my friends, is bizarre. A decade ago, any type of needlework was:

    A. For women only, thus marginalized by association.
    B. For **aged** women, thus further marginalizing the craft.
    C. Just not cool in our disposable culture *("Why make a sweater when you can buy one at Neiman's, oh my gawd!")*

I guarantee you that back then there were no freakin' message boards about any type of needlework, no myriad discussions about frogging (aka, ripping out, as in "Rip it, rip it..."), and not a whole lot of $46, 50-yard hanks of fiber either.

There was Nana and me, hanging out at our local Super Yarn Mart, buying $1 skeins of brightly colored acrylic (the super huge no dyelot skeins with, like, *400 yards* on them) and some big ol' balls of size 30 crochet thread in white or ecru because that is what there was, period.

And Nana was a *great* teacher. I was seven and my first project was a sweater with cables! Yep, cables. Sure I had a few holes here and there, but I was only seven, after all. I didn't make a scarf or a blanket, nothing flat, nothing rectangular and nothing square. Nope, I made a sweater. After that project, I asked my Nana to teach me to crochet. So what does the woman do? She pulls out size 30 thread with what seemed the tiniest hook ever, begins teaching me how to make the smallest chain known to woman, then launches into pineapple-doily mode. With patience I mastered it, and she was with me every step of the way.

Like my Nana, needlework became second-nature to me, both knitting and crochet. I was able to do both interchangeably, and at that time these processes were considered hobbies and not lifestyles.

Although needlework took on a much more important role than mere hobby for me, I never felt the need to define myself as simply either a knitter or crocheter. I mastered both processes, like my Nana, and went about my business.

So, until very recently, I wasn't aware that I needed to pick a more definitive — if simplistic — identity than an artist who is also a crocheter (mostly) who knits (sometimes), but also has a penchant for needlepoint and hand-sewing (though I can machine sew with abandon.)

Embroidery, silk-screening, felting — and not the knit it in wool and wash it in your machine kind of felting either, the real kind with wool shorn right off the sheep that needs to be carded and boiled and stinks like barnyard poo poo — are also not beyond my scope. And I've been known to weave on a floor loom.

No, I guess the next time I go to my LYS and the vegan sheep breeder behind the counter asks what I am making (therefore stating who I am, knitter or crocheter) I should refrain from saying, *"I am crocheting homicidal vegetables donning big bloodshot eyeballs!"* With their $46 a hank fiber.

Instead I will simply reply, "Scarf." Monosyllabic answers are sometimes best. I will leave them wondering whether I am using that cross-over craft crochet or their beloved knitting to make the scarf.

And I will dream of the time when yarn was a lot less expensive and machine-washable, when you could use whatever kind of yarn you wanted, to make whatever kind of item you could dream up, without derision.

I will dream of the time when yarn stores were populated by wrinkle-queens and where the yarn smelled a little like nicotine.

I will dream of the time when yarn was simply YARN, not knitting fiber. I will remember that what I make has merit, whether fashioned by hook, needle or shuttle.

I will embrace those days of yesteryear when we who knit, crochet, sew, weave, felt, needlepoint, and/or embroider were of one tribe, with differing backgrounds, differing paths, who came together at our local Super Yarn Mart to feel-up the acrylic, and we loved it.

And it was good.

Regina Rioux Gonzalez, an exhibiting artist and fabricator of creatures, is obsessed with fairytales, felt and guerrilla vegetables. She received her BA in Art from California State University, Northridge, and her MFA from Claremont Graduate University. Regina spends her days generating income and her nights making art, assembling crocheted churros sporting sombreros and vegetables wielding weapons, and devising ways to unleash them on an unsuspecting world. See them at www.monstercrochet.com

Sock Lessons

Janice Farrell Pea

My mother, Delores Shantz, was born in 1922, the sixth of nine children. Her father was a railroader, many years older than my grandmother whom he met in England during World War I. She had been a young widow with two daughters when he married her and brought her and the girls to the United States. They first lived in Altoona, then moved to Cleveland, where my mother was born. Eventually the growing family moved to Chicago, where my grandmother died after giving birth to her ninth child.

My grandfather, not a young man, was left with two stepdaughters and seven of his own children, the youngest a newborn. The two older girls, Ruth and Eva, returned to England and were lost to our immediate family for many years.

My mother and several of the other children ended up in the warm and tender custody of the State of Illinois. The State placed the newborn and the toddler, both boys, for adoption — without my grandfather's consent. His attempts to remain in touch with his children were thwarted by ostensibly well-meaning officials.

After he died, we found boxes of letters that had been returned to him, as well as letters from officials warning him not to "upset" the children by interfering in their lives.

It was a Dickensian existence. My Aunt Mary, the eldest, managed to keep track of her full siblings. Even though they were divided, they remained a family. My mother passed through various orphanages and foster homes, only finding a permanent home in Bement, Illinois, when she was in high school. Not particularly well treated by the family with whom she lived, she was grateful at least for a home — a real family — safe and secure.

This home also offered her the opportunity to meet the two men who changed her life: The high school principal who saw something in my mother worth saving (he actually falsified her transcript so that she would be admitted into nursing school), and my father. My parents didn't know each other well until dad returned from the army. They married in 1948 and, just over a year later, had me.

Mom didn't speak to me of these things until the mid-sixties, when I was a teenager, the eldest of six children, and she knew she was dying. It explained a lot. For example, I knew that Mom was a bit obsessed with being the "perfect" wife and mother. Every evening, before my father came home from the office, she put on make-up, changed into a dress, and mixed a pitcher of martinis.

I came to understand that she had no model of family life except The Donna Reed Show and Father Knows Best. No one ever taught her to cook, or to sew, or to do any of the other things that most women of her generation took for granted. She was entirely self-taught — and felt that she was never quite good *enough*.

One of her obsessions was lessons — dancing lessons, swimming lessons, classes on etiquette, courses in sewing. If there was a "ladylike" (her word) skill to be learned, she expected me to learn it. She couldn't teach me — so she sent me to class. I learned to make a quilt, dance the waltz, and ride a horse. In 1957, when I was eight, she got it into her head that I should learn how to knit. For some reason, I suggested that she go with me. She agreed.

We went to Linn & Scruggs, a small, family-owned department store of the type that used to exist in every town of reasonable size. On the second floor, there was a Sewing & Notions department, right next to the department that sold Women's Undergarments. In addition to fabric and McCall's patterns, the sewing department also sold yarn, knitting needles, and crochet hooks. The classes were taught by a woman of indeterminate age, with blue-gray hair. I suspected that she was the twin sister of the blue-haired lady with the tape-measure who helped my mother find the right size brassiere.

My first project was a pair of TV slippers. As I recall, these were garter stitch rectangles that were folded and sewn in such a way that they fit the foot. The toe was gathered in a purse string.

One could use bits of felt and pom poms to create bunnies or ducklings. I made gray bunny slippers, with pink felt ears and a white fluffy tail. Googly eyes completed the look. I took to knitting like a duck to water and mastered crochet shortly thereafter.

When I was in high school, my Aunt Mary discovered needlepoint and got me hooked on it as well.

The knitting lady, however, had something totally different in mind for my mother. Mom was given a hank of fine, black yarn and four double-pointed needles. My left-handed mother was supposed to learn the craft of knitting by creating a pair of black wool socks! She worked on them intermittently, without much enthusiasm, and eventually the knitting basket disappeared from the living room. She murmured something about keeping it away from the babies and pets.

In the spring of 1963, my mother went into the hospital to give birth to my youngest brother. Before she came home, she was diagnosed with colon cancer, which had spread to her liver. In 1963 the doctors told her she had three to six months to live. She replied that she had no intention of dying and leaving my father with a house full of preschoolers. How she must have feared our going through what she and her siblings endured! She was true to her word; she hung on until October of 1968.

As the eldest child, one of my tasks was to go through her things and decide what was worth keeping and what should go to Goodwill. I kept several of her purses. My daughter, Katy, found one in my closet last year. So "out," that it's in fashion again, she carries it as she goes off to work in Chicago. I kept Mom's bathrobe, which I wore until it literally fell apart.

There is one thing I regret not keeping. It didn't seem

that important at the time. I found her knitting basket in the back of her closet. In it, there was one, single, misshapen black sock. As far as I could tell, she must have put it down after she began turning the heel. When she picked it up again, she began turning the heel all over again. Instead of the normal L-shaped sock it more closely resembled the letter J. I showed it to my father and his comment was "Isn't that just like your mother, to knit sock for an amputee with a club foot!" We laughed, and cried. Then I put the sad single sock in the discard pile.

What I wouldn't give to have that sock today. I would put it in a shadow box and hang in on my wall. Or maybe I would just carry it around with me so that I could touch it from time to time.

Part of my mother's legacy is my ability to knit. We learned the long-tail cast on together, so it is my preference and I use it for almost every project. When I teach a youngster to knit, as I recently taught my eight-year-old niece, it is what I teach. Every stitch I knit is a tiny link to her. Sometimes, when I am knitting, I carry on conversations with her in my head.

Delores taught me a lot. One of the many things she taught me is the value of passing on our skills to the next generation. And if we weren't lucky enough to have been taught the skill as a child — we can always take lessons!

Janice lives in Champaign, Illinois, with her husband, Bruce, and two dogs. They are enjoying an empty nest now that all four children are grown. Before her graduation from law school at age 47, she had several careers, including owning a yarn shop. She met her husband at her shop when he was a sales representative for a yarn company, and her dearest friends are those she has met through her lifelong obsession with fiber. She notes that her stash of yarn and needlepoint canvasses is enough for several lifetimes.

The Opposite of War

Amie Glasgow

Working the evening shift at a small radio station can be quite lonely. Sure, it sounds like a lot of fun if you turn on the radio, but usually that dj is home alone all day watching tv in their pajamas and then heads off to work just about the time any remnants of a social life are on their way to dinner or parties and conversing with members of the human race.

I found myself in that situation a few years ago: Alone with my cats most days. Social little love bugs that they were, they did nothing to stop my emerging habit of eating everything that would hold still long enough while lying like a lump on the sofa in front of day time television. It became clear that I needed a hobby that would keep me from eating myself out of house and home, or else my hips would soon be so big they wouldn't fit through the door when the eviction notice came...

Right about that time there were a rash of celebrity knitting sightings — Cameron Diaz Taught Julia Roberts How to Knit on the Set of My Best Friends Wedding — Russell Crowe, *"Does He or Doesn't He?"* — Debra Messing, Bridget Fonda, Caroline Rhea, Julianne Moore, Daryl Hannah, Tyra Banks, Sofia Coppola, Camryn Manheim, the list of famous knitters went on and on...

And it occurred to me that it might be tricky to lift a cheese dip laden Dorito to my mouth if both hands were tangled up in yarn.

So off I went to my neighborhood large chain craft-mart. I flipped through their How-To-Knit booklets, picked one and found the recommended supplies (size US 8 green aluminum needles & worsted weight yarn.) Varsity shopper that I am, I traveled the aisles, touching everything in site and loading my basket with a huge palette of yarn colors.

I decided that the best way to handle things was to take them one step at a time, moving on when finally proficient in each procedure. That night, I sat down with the book and struggled through *Casting On*.

I did nothing but cast on for nearly a week. I cast on while talking on the phone, standing on one foot, cooking dinner . I couldn't actually knit a stitch, but I could do a terrific cast on!

The next step; *The Knit Stitch*.

My book offered directions and pictures of the English Standard and Continental methods of holding yarn. A quick read through of the English Standard directions convinced me that I'd need at least three additional hands to master it, so Continental it was. I worked through the knit stitch over and over until I got it right; I could finally knit an entire row without checking the instructions or looking at the pictures. It was September 10, 2001.

The next morning, I awoke to the ringing phone. My boyfriend was calling from work at a naval base in Southern Maryland. *"I'm okay. I don't know when I'll be able to call again. Go turn on the TV. The world just changed."*

Along with the rest of the world, I sat in front of the television, tears streaming down my face. But I had knitting. Along with the myriad colors in that great pile of yarn I had bought there was some red, white, and blue. I knit, and I knit. In my mind I kept hearing words from a favorite musical of mine, <u>Rent</u>, "*The opposite of war isn't peace. It's creation."*

I couldn't stop the war. But I had yarn, I had needles, I had knitting. I could create.

After her nationally-noted start in knitting, Amie threw herself into fiber whole-hog (should that be "whole sheep"?) and now is teaching spinning and knitting, as well as occasional commission design work.

She still works in radio full-time, but is pleased to add "cancer survivor" to her resume. Amie lives with her husband, part-time stepson, and a zoo-full of beloved animals near Baltimore, MD. Read more from her online at rosebyany.blogspot.com.

Tracy

Amy Pezzoni

I taught myself how to knit out of a book last June.

It was a rough time for our family. My brother's girlfriend had been diagnosed almost four years earlier with Type B Non-Hodgkin's Nodular Lymphoma now in the most advanced stage.

Tracy was special to everyone who knew her. She had a smile for all, even on her worst days. A wonderful mother, Tracy loved her daughter very much. My brother was transformed when Tracy entered his life; he moved from an existence of drugs and crime to one of love and parenting. He and Tracy had begun dating when she was pregnant, he had been Daddy to her daughter since before she was born.

Tracy was a fighter. She had long held the cancer at bay. Every year she would be proclaimed clear of the cancer, only to discover six months later it had returned. She and my brother would have married, but that would have meant losing her medical coverage. My brother could not afford her bills, and she would not have received the excellent medical treatment that allowed her three and a half more years with her daughter. Tracy's treatments started the day after her daughter turned one.

My own immediate family was going away to a cabin for a few days and I needed a solo activity. I had always wanted to learn to knit, so along came my learn-to-knit book. I completed a dishcloth pattern, then I decided to challenge myself with my next project; a baby blanket I had seen online. The repeating hourglass pattern would be fantastic practice for me, so I cast on and began knitting. About the time we returned from our trip, Tracy began to go downhill quickly.

Upon our return we saw Tracy for her birthday. She was dying. It was hard to find a card that didn't mention the next year or how horrible birthdays were, but I found one that said, Consider this a hug with a crease in the middle. Tracy spent her birthday in bed, on oxygen, itching terribly from the cancer. She looked so tired, so drained from her long fight and required frequent blood transfusions.

Working on the blanket my thoughts were constantly with Tracy. As I knitted, I raged about her disease. How could a young mother be forced to go through something so horrible? How could she be taken from her bright beautiful daughter, and not be able to see her grow up? She will never see the milestones that other parents can't take for granted. I cried into that blanket many times.

The blanket slowly came to belong to Tracy. I started knitting as fast as my beginner hands would let me. I made several mistakes along the way, but was too inexperienced and in too much of a hurry to go back and fix them. Since I had decided that this blanket was Tracy's, I needed to give it to her.

I did not know how much time I had, so I just had to go as quickly as possible.

I kept telling myself I would stop with the next hourglass repeat, but was driven to keep going. The pattern called for seven skeins of yarn, but when I was almost finished with the fourth I received word that Tracy's vitals had cut in half. This was it for her, it was a matter of hours.

I made arrangements for someone to watch my son and grabbed the blanket in progress. My plan was to finish off the blanket right where I was and give it to her. Five minutes into the drive to the hospital 45 minutes away, I called my step-mom to let her know I was on the way. They, too, were on their way to the hospital, but my brother had just called her to tell her that Tracy had passed. It was impossible to drive with my eyes filled with tears of grief; I pulled into the nearest parking lot and cried.

I was sad and angry. I didn't know what to do with myself, so I just cried against the steering wheel and thought of Tracy. Memories of her began to surface and I let them wash over me. I called my friend who was watching my son, and told her the news. When she asked if there was anything she could do, I asked if she would light a candle for Tracy.

Thinking about that candle helped me regain enough control to drive safely to the hospital to be there for my brother and her family. At one point I mentioned the blanket to my brother and he told me that she didn't need it anymore.

I finished off the blanket that night. It crossed my mind to complete the entire blanket, but I knew that it would be too painful, and that I would be tempted to put it away. It was important to me that I finish it, even half done. When I saw her daughter a few weeks later, I handed her the blanket. I told her that I had made it for her mommy, and since her mommy couldn't use it, I hoped she would take care of it for her — that she would snuggle with the blanket and remember the love of her mother and our family.

She accepted the blanket and pointed out a star in the night sky. She told me, *"That's the first star of the night, Mommy said that first star would be her watching over me."*

Amy Pezzoni, a Computer Engineer in another life, was inspired by Tracy's blanket to continue knitting. As mother to two-year-old Andrew and wife to Kevin, she has found much knitting support at the Wooly Wonder Forums, www.woolywonder.com. Look for her chatting up the fiber!

Proof of Life

Mary Anne Mitchell

Knitting was the solace I embraced when my life took a wrong turn and I was stricken with Chronic Fatigue Syndrome. I was a passive knitter during my healthy years, grabbing moments in my busy life to knit a few rows here and there, leaving my uncompleted projects lingering in the yarn basket with no end in sight.

To create something with my hands was as vital to my emotional and physical health as sleep and fresh air. When I was a child, not a day went by when I wasn't drawing, writing, sewing or dreaming up a new way to express who I was and who I wanted to become. I learned to knit at the age of 14 from my grandmother. I was fascinated by the simplicity of the tools and threw myself into the world of knitting with the same passion I brought to everything at that age. Then I discovered boys and knitting took a backseat to real life.

It wasn't until I became ill and unable to move from my bed that my hands itched for the feel of wool and the soothing click of knitting needles. It had been many years since I had done any serious knitting, but my fingers needed no retraining or coaching.

They fell into the rhythm of knit one, purl one with the ease of an old friend come to pay a long overdue visit.
Although I was suffering most days with relentless exhaustion and severe vertigo, the simple act of

knitting became a touchstone; a soothing link to the life I inhabited before illness. Through many traumatic moments I would pick up my knitting and escape inward, weaving the pieces of my broken life together with the knit and purl stitches. When I felt so sick I couldn't get out of bed for days at a stretch, I kept my knitting in a kit beside me and would work a few stitches at a time, stopping when I felt too weak or dizzy.

As the months, and then years, have slipped slowly by, my health has languished in a paralyzing half-life; a stasis that often leaves me feeling unplugged from the universe. In the ensuing silence, I have turned to my knitting for comfort. The act of knitting has become my mantra, and a defense against the darkness of spirit I have felt nibbling away at the edge of my consciousness.

Knitting has been a way for me to give something from my heart and hands to others at a time when the simplest physical act takes immense effort. I have used my knowledge of yarn and needles to create tangible objects that can be seen and touched, proof that I am still able to contribute in some small way to the world that seems to be rushing past me on high alert. Through online knitting groups and forums, I have been able to stay connected with a vibrant community of creative and caring individuals, many of whom I now call friend.

Knitting is my therapy — in a very real sense. I feel blessed to still have the ability to hold two sticks and some string. I live with hope that my health will improve, and that I will return to the physically active life I once led.

But regardless of the outcome, I know I will always be grateful for the joy that knitting has brought to my life.

Before retirement from a federal government agency in 2000 for health reasons, Mary Ann and her husband led an active life of cycling, hiking, camping and motorbiking across the Western US and Oregon Coast. Gratified that she is surrounded with friends and family who support her through her illness, Mary Ann lives a life filled with love and acceptance. These days she can be found listening to stories on the computer while knitting or reading emails and chatting with friends online. She writes under the name Miss Woolly Knits at http://knittingbunny.blogspot.com

The Best Defense

is a lot of yarn...

Amy Polcyn

So maybe I had lost my mind. My daughter was deeply entrenched in the terrible twos, I had just returned to work full-time after a stint as a stay-at-home mom, and one morning I woke up and decided it was time to go back to school and get a master's degree. Whether it was a sudden attack of ambition or just the sleep deprivation talking, I signed up for a full load of classes.

Needless to say, I was in over my head. The typical day went something like this: Wake up, take daughter to day care, wrangle first and second graders until 3:45, pick up daughter, pretend to make dinner, ignore housework, read many pages in textbooks, check papers, complete assignments, plan lessons, collapse at kitchen table, wake up in middle of night with imprint of book edge on cheek, stumble into bed still wearing work clothes. I knew I couldn't go on like this.

What to do? I'm not a This-wasn't-a-very-good-idea, maybe-I-should-rethink-it kind of person. When I decide to do something, it gets done. The plan could not be abandoned. Still, I needed help. Strangely enough, the solution came through finding something to take up even more of my time: Knitting!

At the time I was a casual knitter. I had been knitting for about a year or so and had finished a few scarves and a sweater that would never fit anyone. I thought if I had something easy and fun to knit, it might be relaxing enough to keep me sane while I dealt with my crazy schedule. The next Saturday I went yarn shopping, and $80 later I had a nice assortment of yarn to play with. I cast on for a hat that afternoon.

As I worked the stitches, round and round the circular needle, I began to feel the tension in my shoulders release. My mind drifted to a calm and happy place where there were no students, no textbooks, no papers to write. I felt like me again.

Granted, the students, textbooks, and papers still existed and were waiting for me once I set down my needles. Somehow, though, it didn't seem to bother me as much as it had before. I had taken a little yarn vacation, and was ready to face the long days and nights ahead.

Over the next two years, I finished a lot of projects. When I look back at them, each reminds me of a different course, a different paper. The statistical analysis socks. The research scarves. The thesis sweater. Each stitch is a page read, a word typed, a sleepless night.

I made it to graduation, and resumed a reasonably normal life. The knitting has remained, even grown, helping me to get through life's little crises just as it kept me sane then.

In my little fortress of solitude I rebuild myself each evening, shedding the stresses of the day like a lizard's skin.

I emerge renewed, reborn, and ready for anything — especially more knitting.

Amy Polcyn lives in Livonia, Michigan, where she has been knitting obsessively since 2000. When forced to relinquish her needles, she teaches gifted first- and second-graders, enjoys the company of her family, and occasionally engages in housework. Amy is also a knitwear designer with several patterns in print (and more to come!) She chronicles her knitting and designing progress at frottez.blogspot.com.

Snowflakes & Scarves

Kate McKiernan

As I sat looking out at the large flakes swaying towards the ground, I was reminded of an itchy green scarf. It wasn't the soft green color you see in the stores today, but the signature of the seventies: avocado green. My daughter, home during winter break, was next to me once again exclaiming her boredom.

"Come on, I'm going to teach you to knit," I said as we rushed up the stairs to face the depths of my closet. Buried under numerous cross-stitch patterns and crochet hooks was a scarf I started myself, over fifteen years earlier. This scarf traveled from Florida to New York and four subsequent moves after that. It had history and memories, but overall, it screamed, Incompletion!

I took a deep breath, aimed the scissors and snipped. Gone. My eight-year-old cheered as I said goodbye to procrastination and fear of public ridicule for admitting I liked to knit. I am, after all, entering my fortieth year. It is about time I do things because I want to and refuse to allow others to dictate how I should live my life.

An hour later the snow had stopped falling and the roads were wet with its memory. Our knitting lesson was a huge success as one didn't want to relinquish the needles to the other. Being that aforementioned maturing adult, I made the executive decision to jump in the car and head to the local craft store.

Later that day, as we sat happily by the window watching yet another quiet snowfall, I told my daughter the *Story of the Green Scarf.*

I was seven or eight, looking out of the window onto Holland Avenue. The snow was falling, and I was staying overnight at my grandparents' house. I went to the kitchen to tell my grandmother — affectionately known as Mom Allen — that I had nothing to do. Her blue eyes laughed as she said it was about time to take a break, anyway. We sat on the couch, her calm, quiet voice telling me how to hold the yarn, explaining the difference between knitting and purling. Mom Allen told me stories about her own mothers' knitting and how, when she was young, most girls my age already knew how to knit. I was fascinated! How old fashioned this was, it was so cool!

As we knit I told my daughter about my introduction to knitting, and subsequent attempts at resuming the craft. *"It doesn't matter if you stop knitting at some point. Life gets busy."* I told my daughter.

But someday — perhaps as she sits with her daughter or granddaughter — she may remember the collective warmth of hot chocolate, yarn, clicking needles and mom, and want to recapture the peace and tranquility of those memories.

Mom Allen is no longer with us, though every time I pick up my needles I am reminded of how I got there. Now, my daughter and I make memories of our own.

One day she, too, will tell the *Story of the Green Scarf,* and add her own *Tale of the Patriotic Coaster,* weaving together generations of love.

Kate was born and raised in Albany, NY and lives in the area now with her husband Mark and daughter, Kelly. As a young child, she'd often stay overnight at her grandparents home, enjoying the clicking of Mom Allen's long metal needles.

Family Knitting Ties

Kate Giali

When I began my knitting journey, I never would have guessed the impact it would have in my life. My knitting has become a form of meditation, and surprisingly has brought my family and friends closer to me. The act of knitting itself has become a natural relaxant; as each stitch is created I become more centered.

I have invented my own knitting meditation for times when I am overwhelmed: With each stitch I make, I recite a positive word: peace, joy, love, healing, abundance, hope, relax, etc. This usually moves me to a calm state of bliss, and I have been able to work through problems I am having with myself and others. My own way of escaping an otherwise hectic, crazy day.

The more I knit, the more family and friends commented on it. Most told me that they would like to learn, yet I didn't feel comfortable teaching them myself. While taking a Sweater 101 class at my local knitting shop, however, I came up with the idea of organizing a private knitting class for some of my family and close friends.

I approached the teacher, Jeannine, who was so patient and talented that I knew she would be an excellent choice. She agreed and, Voila! Our Family Knitters Group was formed! Through our regular lessons I have become closer to friends & family members and have made wonderful new friends in the process. After a stressful day our Biweekly Family & Friends Knitting Night is a perfect retreat. We not only form strong bonds with each other, but we have created a great support system as we talk, laugh, and knit for a few hours every other week.

The feelings that stir in me, as I watch our class grow into knitters, are amazing. Each knitter is accomplished in their own unique way. Witnessing the look on the face of a new knitter when they have mastered a technique, or finished a project, is a wonderful experience. I have never received more out of any hobby or craft as I have from knitting. It is hard at this point to imagine a day without the peace I draw from my needles and yarn.

Kate is an aspiring writer, crafter and established knitting fanatic. She lives with her husband in Upstate NY, where they are surrounded by amazing family and friends.

Backtracking

Annie Modesitt

When I was a girl my mother took a job as a delivery person. We were in a tight financial situation so my middle-class mom, who had supported her family in her youth but who hadn't held a job in 20 years, began looking for work. She could type and take dictation better than any 25-year-old, but with no secretarial openings available mom took a job delivering coupons for a photographic studio. I remember how tired she would be after a long day at work, depressed that no one would give her a secretarial job because of her age. She was 55 and she was worn out.

On days off from school I would run deliveries for her. I would be her legs; walking to the doors, dropping off booklets and collecting payment while she watched me from the car. It was fun for me and a relief for her. To have ten minutes of sitting when she might have been climbing stairs and knocking on doors was a tiny luxury I could give her.

To develop my sense of direction mom would let me be the navigator. I'd look up addresses in the city map booklet and arrange our deliveries in the most sensible route. Mom's only firm rule was, *No Backtracking!*

Time was short and she didn't want to retrace our steps. It became a mantra in our family, the eleventh commandment, *Thou shalt not BACKTRACK!*

Generally I chose short, point-to-point trips, but sometimes I would digress and send us down the same road twice. The tightening of my mother's hands on the steering wheel was her only admonishment.

The problem was that I *enjoyed* backtracking. I liked seeing the same street twice from a different direction. The voyeur in me delighted in glimpsing families unloading a car, carrying groceries into the house, then seeing the same family twenty minutes later swinging on their front porch with glasses of iced tea. I would wave, they'd wave back, mom would grip the wheel and drive on.

I have heard of some knitters who never need to unknit, to rip out, to frog (*rip-it, rip-it* in the cyber-knit vernacular) but I'm not one of them. There are times when I'd like to achieve this super-human power to never unravel. Believe me, it's not fun to undo what you've spent hours (or days) knitting. But accidents happen — at least they do to me. Life and creativity also happen, and not always on schedule.

I'm a fast knitter; not necessarily because my hands work at lightning speed, but because I've learned to be very efficient in my movements and to take shortcuts that don't impact my final knit fabric. It is by ripping out, and deconstructing my rip outs, that I've been able to mistress these efficiencies.

When I attempt a difficult stitch pattern or bobble technique and then rip it out, I'm in a wonderful position to dissect what I've done from several angles. *Ah!* I think to myself, *THAT'S how those loops fall together to make that pattern!* and then I take it a step further, *If I move these loops in THIS direction, or work this part backwards, it will create a totally different but complimentary pattern!* Instead of cursing my inadequacy as a knitter that led to the ripping, I try to embrace the opportunity to learn more about the stitches that are falling apart in my hands.

I will rip out many rows in my life. Facing this truism head-on has made life easier. People knit and learn in different ways, some pick up techniques immediately, almost effortlessly. Others pay for every skill with toil, sweat and sometimes tears.

My mother and I were stubborn in different ways, so we learned our lessons differently. If my mother had been a knitter I'm certain she seldom would have needed to rip out. I, however, have come to believe that ripping out is good for the soul — it keeps us humble.

And, I must admit, I rather enjoy the quiet little *pop, pop, pop* of the yarn as the loops fall out of the previous row of stitches. It's an antithetical feeling of accomplishment, similar to the exhilaration my kids feel when they pop the cells in the sheets of plastic bubble wrap I hide in my office. I don't knit for the fun of ripping out, but as long as I must rip out, why not enjoy the small physical pleasure that comes with it?

I will admit, though, that at times I leave items which need to be *unknit* sitting on my table for a week before I can steel myself to tear out the faulty rows.

If mistakes are part of being human, then I am very, very human. In a perfect world there would be no ripping out. But I don't live in a perfect world, I live in *my* world, so rip I must!

What I learned from my childhood of running deliveries is that a straight line — while always the shortest route between two points — is not always the fastest route. Backtracking allowed me to find alternative, quicker routes that might not have been immediately obvious.

In time I began running deliveries on my own during high school summers when my mother moved into a management position at her job. All of those hours memorizing one-way streets and short cuts paid off when I had time to slip into an afternoon movie and still make it back to the office before my deadline.

Several years ago my husband, children and I drove across the country to visit my mom. Several times we got lost, and spent more time visiting relatives and friends on the way than we'd anticipated. We had to forego some planned side trips. While my kids watched videos in the backseat, the dog slept, my husband drove and I knit the last of the gift socks. It was a good trip.

Driving from New Jersey to Texas and back, knitting socks as gifts, ripping out and actually *enjoying* the process — these things may make no sense to many folks. They don t have to, they make sense to me.

Annie Modesitt is a hand knit designer and craft writer. This essay first was published by Interweave Knits magazine.

Knitting Sisterhood

Grace S. Peng

I knit to meet other women.

That may sound strange coming from a happily married wife and mother, but I work in a heavily male-dominated field. At my last job, I spent entire workdays without interaction with other women. I spend long hours in front of a computer, or with pen and paper. So when work is finished, I long for tactile experiences such as knitting and sewing.

In fact, the first thing I did when I obtained my current job, a thousand miles away from my last home, was to surf the internet for knitting and quilting guilds. I found both, even before my move. Many of my current friends are fellow guild members and, through them, I feel part of a large community of women. I doubt that I would have felt at home here as quickly without my local quilting and knitting guilds.

From the beginning, I used knitting to connect with other women. I learned how to knit during a summer exchange program in Germany. Alone in a foreign country, I watched with envy the groups of girls sitting, chatting and knitting.

I befriended a classmate by asking her to teach me how to knit, and quickly became obsessed with the craft. My passion returned home with me, and soon my sister and my mother also were knitting.

Unlike sewing, which I do at home tethered to my heavy sewing machine, knitting is portable. I can knit almost anywhere. Whenever I knit in public, people come up to talk to me. Conversations begin with the knitting, but can take off in any direction.

People say that they want to learn how to knit or they tell me about their works in progress (*WIPs*.) Sometimes men will come up to me and reminisce about their mother or grandmother's knitting.

But I also enjoy knitting alone at the beginning or end of my day. When I knit, I think about all of the anonymous women throughout history who also have knitted. When I solve a sweater design or construction problem, I wonder how many other women were confronted with the same problem and what kind of solutions they found. I feel a tribal affiliation with those long-gone creative problem solvers. They didn't worry about being hip — they lived, they toiled, and they made useful and beautiful things out of whatever resources that they had.

During college, however, knitting fell by the wayside. As good yarn shops became more difficult to find — and with three excellent fabric shops close by — I gravitated towards sewing and quilting. But I hadn't entirely forsaken my love of knitting, which I rediscovered when, as a new mom, I visited a co-worker who was expecting her first child.

She showed me two beautiful sweaters that she had knit from patterns in *'Wee Knits'*. The pattern book came home with me that day, and within the week I became a regular at my LYS (*local yarn shop.*)

Like many women, I had fantasies about motherhood. I was going to be one of those moms that read to her child every night, regardless of work and life pressures, or just plain bad days. After a difficult pregnancy and birth, though, I became severely ill and developed asthma. Difficulty breathing in the evenings made reading aloud at bedtime pretty much impossible, so I took up knitting and sewing with a vengeance. I couldn't read my daughter to sleep at night, but I could wrap her in hand knit sweaters. After returning to my job, as I dropped my daughter off at day-care each morning, I left her in the embrace of mommy-made outfits.

My sister and I have moved around the country for various reasons (education, career, husbands' careers.) We drifted apart. But when she found out that I had taken up knitting again, my sister told me about her own fiber arts blog. We have come full circle, and the passion that we share binds us.

She even created an account so that I can make guest appearances on her blog. Now we always know what the other has on her needles.

Perhaps most satisfying of all, knitting allows me to enjoy the products of my labor. Housework is never done. But, when the last stitch is bound off and all the yarn ends woven in, a garment is finished and my work is done — at least, until my daughter's next growth spurt.

In one of her earliest memories, Grace sat near a sunny window and alternately scrunched up and smoothed down a piece of cotton fabric, watching the play of light and shadow and feeling the smoothness of the fabric. She has been experimenting with textiles, color and texture ever since. In 2000, she became chief couturier to her daughter, Iris. Along the way, she earned a BA in Mathematics, a BS in Chemistry, and a PhD in Chemical Physics, and married a spectroscopist. Her day job in satellite meteorology and numerical weather prediction is just as much fun as her fiber arts hobbies. She lives with her family near Los Angeles.

I knit my way out of my shell

Ellen R Margulies

I was born shy, passing my formative years hidden (cowering) behind my mom's skirt, until I was too large to actually be hidden — even by my mother's formidable hips.

All through public school I perfected my secret power of invisibility. In high school and college, I'd choose the seat in the darkest corner of the last row to hide out for forty-five minutes. No one knew I was there. If I actually worked up the courage to take an aerobics or yoga course, you'd never be able to pick me out in a line-up. I lead a stealth life, undercover: a Jewish ninja.

It seemed logical that I would be attracted to knitting. I could sit at home, just me and my lovely skeins of yarn, quietly knitting and purling the hours away. A few years ago, an online knitting buddy emailed me about a Stitch 'N Bitch group starting up here in Los Angeles. Sounded nice, but the chances of Ms. Invisible going were pretty remote. I wondered if I should scope out the place first to plan my escape route, in case I was too shy to connect with anyone.

Okay, that was too crazy, even for me, so I decided to take a chance and go. I was the first to arrive (to make it easier to do my disappearing act.) But as each new knitter arrived, yarn and needles peeking from their totes, I found myself growing more relaxed, compelled to stay. That's when things got interesting. We each took out our projects, and there was an immediate connection — as if we all shared the same secret language: *FOs, WIPs, Frogging, Intarsia, Entrelac†*

But I crossed an even greater hurdle. This was the first time in twenty years that I actually had knit in front of another human being. Suddenly, I was visible again.

I joined Weight Watchers recently (those formidable hips run in the family!) and I noticed one of the members knitting before the meeting. The yarn she was using was so gorgeous, I just had to ask about it. There was that instant bond again, as we gabbed nonstop about our favorite yarns, shops and designers.

I was almost sorry the meeting had to start, because it meant we had to stop our fiber talk. Eventually other knitters started bringing their projects and we all had a mini show-n-tell each week before the meeting. I was so chatty in our little club, it spilled over into the meeting. Now everyone there knows my name.

I'm permanently out of the shadows now. I've been a receptionist, a teacher and I've even done a bit of public speaking. I'm finally living life in the front row and enjoying every minute of it. All it took was my love of two sticks and some string to change my life forever.

†FO: Finished Object; WIPs Works in progress; Frogging: Ripping out; Intarsia: A form of colorwork; Entrelac: A form of basketweave knitting

Ellen is a born and bred New Yawka from Sheepshead Bay, Brooklyn, who moved to Los Angeles with her husband and daughter 10 years ago. Although it's tough to find good bagels or pizza in L.A., there are some fabulous yarn shops where it's possible to get quite a satisfactory fiber fix.

Me, and...

Drew Emborsky

Life - at least into my twenties - had always been about *me*.

I was happy, I seemed to get things done, and that was all that concerned *me*. I lived in an exotic foreign country, had a high-paying powerful job and many friends. On paper life looked good. I had a life that others would envy, which seemed like the most important thing in the world.

As my own personal *me* decade drew to a close and my thirtieth birthday was imminent, I found myself with an overwhelming desire to be nearer to my family. Having no reason *not* to return to the US, I listened to my inner voice, packed up and prepared myself for a typical, wonderful, homecoming. After all, this was *me,* and good things had a way of coming *my* way.

When I returned to the States, however, everything changed quite suddenly.

My mom – who was my closest friend – passed away suddenly one day. There was no warning, it was unexpected – a hard slap. I had no way of knowing how this experience would change every aspect of my life.

Existence at once changed from being all about *me* to being all about *nothing*.

Grief will make a heart ponder. After brooding, reflecting, hashing and rehashing – crying sometimes for hours at a stretch – I made a discovery that put my earlier ambition into perspective.

The striving for success in my twenties had really been all about *Mom* and not just me. I was trying as hard as I could to make a positive impression on *Mom*. Quite simply, my heart's desire was to make my mother proud. Now that I was without her, I found myself lethargic - almost dormant. I was barely able to get through each day. But somehow the days passed.

As I was well on my way to full out hermit-hood (which is a whole other story) I was forwarded an email from a friend. It discussed a charity which was accepting donated crocheted afghan squares. Now, I'm a handy guy, like my siblings I've known how to crochet since childhood and even had a few random hooks lying around the apartment.

I clicked on a link to the charity's website (www.heartmadeblessings.org), read the submission requirements, and figured it would be a nice way to pass some time. What I couldn't foresee was how profoundly I would be affected by a small unselfish act like crocheting afghan squares.

First I made squares by following the same pattern over and over, repeating the same stitch pattern and sequence of hand movements, allowing my fingers to memorize the motif. This repetition calmed my mind and quieted the negative thoughts that had played nonstop for so long. Ironically, when I was practically hibernating my mind raced with pain; now that I was busily running fiber through my fingers at breakneck speed, my mind was at peace. I began by feeling that I was doing a charitable deed, but it soon became clear that I was getting far more from each square I fashioned than I could have dreamed.

New ideas for squares came to me − original, inventive, joyful inspirations. I was unprepared for the fertility springing from my brain! After so many years of constantly feeling blue and numb, it was unusual to experience enthusiastic emotions − happy, creative thoughts.

I fed upon this new buoyant way of feeling and it became a driving force in my life. Crochet was taking me in directions I could never have imagined, and I was happy to be along for the ride.

There was discernible change in my personality and outlook. It was as if a dam of good feelings had broken inside my heart, washing over my entire being. Crochet was literally my therapy and my salvation. I found myself laughing easily, living joyfully and looking optimistically towards the future.

And I can't help but reflect that *Mom* had taught me to crochet. This is her gift to *me*.

Drew Emborsky (The Crochet Dude) has crocheted since the age of five. He studied fine art at Kendall College of Art & Design in Grand Rapids, MI. Drew is a national member of the Crochet Guild of America where he received his Master's certificate in May, 2005. His publications can be found at www.lulu.com/thecrochetdude. Drew resides in Houston, Texas with his two cats Chandler & Cleocatra.

Wade in the Yarn

Melissa Shaw

I'm incredibly grateful to a woman named Janice, for inviting me to a weekly lunchtime knitting group at work, and for teaching me — in such a *patient* manner — to knit. Her effect on my life, on my mental health, has been immeasurable.

My skill set is growing, both in knitting and in my ability to manage the many hard blows that life deals. I am not able to expand my knitting knowledge by force, I am someone who must ease gently into a new skill, dipping a toe in the knitting waters, wading in a bit at a time.

In life, as in knitting, it is important to know yourself and be true to that awareness. I know that I have issues with my attention span, and I have come to accept that I can become very frustrated when a project goes on for too long. There is so much variety inherent in the knitting process that I'm able to select simple projects that I can complete within a reasonable amount of time, while still reaping the benefits of the experience. Knitting is portable therapy. I can fit it into my schedule whenever I need, wherever I am — except when I'm driving!

I'm glad that knitting has become trendy, it's much easier to find resources for yarn and tools, but I'm not jumping up and down to knit the project-of-the-moment. I knit things only if I think someone actually can use them, or if the item involves a process or knitting experience I think I'll enjoy.

I wish I'd known Janice, or someone like her , before my mother was diagnosed with cancer. A soft, comfy chemo cap would have been a blessing to her cancer ravaged scalp.

As soon as I learned about the existence of such a thing as a chemo cap, I ordered yarn and a pattern and put myself to work. I had not yet worked on circular needles, but a simple project and a definite goal made this skill easier for me to master. The idea that I was helping to ease the suffering of other cancer victims also helped me better understand my own mothers' suffering, and heal a bit of myself.

Like so many knitters, I have yet to complete a project for me. My gift to myself has been the joy of sharing my knitted products, a deep source of happiness. Two chemo caps have gone to a friend-of-a-friend, a few preemie hats have been knit for a local hospital, and, of course, numerous knitted hats and scarves grace the heads and necks of friends and family members.

Recently a new health crisis loomed on our family's horizon, and knitting has been a calming grace. My father has had five or six surgeries — I've honestly lost count — leading to the loss of his right leg.

I desperately needed a way to be productive — to be occupied — while sitting for hours at a time in the hospital. Knitting filled that need. Thank you Janice.

Every time a surgery is scheduled, I'm ready in the waiting room, with a novel and a knitting project or two. Knitting keeps my hands busy, gives my mind a release from so much medical jargon. My worries fade a bit, and at the end of the day I have something to show for my time. Those waiting-room chairs are still uncomfortable, but I'm able to tolerate them a bit easier because I'm not just sitting and watching the clock. I carry my project bag with me everywhere I go and knit when I'm stuck at train crossings, and even during informal meetings at work.

I am all in favor of people learning to knit in whatever way is most comfortable for them. My sister-in-law recently used a book to teach herself to knit Continental style, holding her yarn in her left hand. While some people might insist that she learn the right way, I marvel at how much faster she is! I tried this method myself when a shoulder injury threatened to stall my pre Christmas projects, and my knitting flowed much easier. It makes me ask myself, How can knitting be therapy if it's forced? Who is to decide which is the right way to knit?

While the act of knitting is therapeutic, knitting for others is, for me, advanced therapy (although I do hope to knit something for myself someday!)

Melissa describes herself as "a little bit hyperactive — quite the multi-tasker." A big fan of wooden knitting needles and good yarn, Melissa someday hopes to make a sweater. A training & communications specialist and co-director of the Crazy Cat Ladies Society (www.crazycatladies.org) Melissa lives in Michigan with her husband John and blogs about life at www.livejournal.com /users/crazycatladymel.

Rough Edges

holly christmas

my core was ripped out by the blast. in the weeks that followed, my mind numbed, but the gaping hole remained.

the numbness fades, the edges of the hole still raw. i feel each nerve and cell collapsing, withdrawing from the comfortable numbness which protected me for so long. i sleep.

activities of the past do not allow me to remain awake. japanese class throws me down a pit of memories. the instructor's mouth moves, but i cannot hear her, the pit is too deep. i study at home and each minute brings up shovels of earth as i attempt to hide myself, sink further into the darkness, hide from the light that forces me awake each day.

i lie in bed. my feet twist and turn while the rest of me hides in the covers. i do not understand why i have to wake up every single day . please just let me fade, let me disappear into the pit. two sticks and some string. i walk along, past the place we said good-bye, and move toward the pit. then i come across the two sticks and string, and stay where i am.

i lie in bed, feet twitching, dreading the day, the awakeness of it all. i sink into the pit, but now there is a layer of knitted items at the bottom, and two sticks and some string.

i pick up stitches at the edges left behind by the blast, knitting sections where chunks have gone missing. the hole gapes a bit less, the edges not quite as raw. those that are still rough now have cozies protecting them, because it makes me laugh to think that my nerves need cozies, and I miss laughing.

two sticks and some string. i walk past the point where we decided he should go to the hospital. i head to the pit. not as deep now, light seeps in over the edge and weaves itself into the knitted fabric on the bottom. i pick up the sticks and string and am just there, with the light and the yarn and the pain.

i lie in bed, feet twirling, dreading the day. but if i get up now, i can do one row before work — and maybe start to unravel the cozy enveloping my soul.

i walk past the point where he told me he would miss the smell of the air, where i knew he would not turn back, and i run for the pit , fall, and land in the cushion of knit-ness as the light bounces off its surface, limning the beauty and pain and hopefulness of it all. and i am just there, with and without the pain and the sorrow, with and without the joy. i am just there: me and my two sticks and string.

holly has at least one too many interests and currently is looking for more

Healing Circles

Nancy Duffy

One hot summer night I couldn't sleep. Instead of tossing in bed I got up and began crocheting. I crocheted a chain, which became a ring, which became a circle — then two — then four circles, and on and on. It was fitting. As a member of an incest survivors group the circles seemed to me to represent a journey toward healing.

The circles evolved into crocheted bottle carriers and backpacks. Someone in the survivors group guided me toward Inspirations, a creative healing circle for women, survivors, in the psychiatric community.

Inspirations became one of the most positive influences in my life. Each member had at one time in her life been kicked to the ground, but we refused to stay down. We found strength in our circle. The impact we had on each other in our creative circle was tangible and life lasting.

My creative path was fiber; some women painted, others formed beautiful pottery or found different outlets to sustain them. Our ability to create as a group enabled some of us to reduce our medications and emergency medical visits. Slowly we began to overcome many of our fears and self doubts; we became confident, supported by the gifts each woman brought to our creative circle. We became proud, we became daring.

We offered our pieces for sale at craft markets, and they sold! The positive feedback our work received was new for many of us. Learning to receive it gracefully was difficult, but an important step in our healing. Our work was worthwhile, therefore we were worthwhile, a stunning insight for many in our circle.

At Inspirations we were all one. We were an amazing group: from homeless women dwelling in shelters to those more fortunate with more permanent housing, even their own apartments. Our education varied as well. For many of us, violence led us to the mental health system. We discovered a sisterhood of unlikely souls at Inspirations.

In the way of many tenuously funded programs, Inspirations lasted only two or three years. Funding difficulties and political differences led to its demise, several of the participants have since passed away. However, my experience with Inspirations gave me belief in myself and my creativity. I've drawn on this well of strength often in the past 10 years, since the dissolution of Inspirations.

My tenure with Inspirations marked the beginning of a long, painful healing journey from which I am currently emerging. Life can seem overwhelming at times; without my yarn and fibers to play with I wonder if I would have made it this far.

At times I have been suicidal. Drowning in darkness, I would reach out to my stash and grab onto the lifeline of an undiscovered treasure.

What a waste it would be to die and not make something with this yarn. My fiber, my stash, a part of me that had not yet lived!

It is not just the yarn and a hook or needle; it is the color, the texture, the touch of the fiber. I work from feeling. The spark of an idea may spring from a pattern, but my work quickly takes on a form of its own and takes me away from my pain. ALL the pain: physical; emotional; psychological. The arthritic crone and the terrified two year old — whoever is present, she is freed from her pain once she is able to connect with her fiber and create.

Creating a whole from a string, sometimes just bits and pieces of string, heals me. Unraveling sweaters when I can't knit is a form of meditation; I contemplate the unraveling of my life. And then I re-create magical shawls from the colorful bits and pieces, as I put the bits and pieces of my life back together.

Not all projects are completed. Life changes so quickly, or is so painful, that at times just starting a project serves a purpose.

Some items do get finished, but ripping out becomes part of the process. A meditative rehashing of what had been done, a reflection of what may need to be reworked before moving on.

The anxious little girl who hid behind closed doors and drawn curtains — full of fear when she wanted to create — is no longer afraid; she is out there in the world.

With a lot of hard work and the help from the women of Inspirations, she released her creativity, plied her fibers, and found herself.

Nancy is a self taught fiber artist/craftsperson.

Yarn Flings & the Real Thing

Dawn Penny

I actually started knitting when I was a teen.

In my usual way of doing anything throughout my life, my first teenage knitting crush was begun with a pattern way over my head and deep, black yarn. Perhaps the instructions were too difficult, perhaps I treasured my eyesight more than I needed a hand knit black sweater, but the unfinished sweater remained hidden for years. I finally threw the bag of assorted cardigan parts away just before I started knitting again — in my 30s.

My second knitting fling began with another of my typical MO's; competition with my identical twin sister. She was pregnant and on bed rest, knitting for her soon-to-be-born son. This time there was no sack of errant bits of sweater shoved in my closet a few months into my knitting spree — I truly, deeply loved knitting and I couldn't stop. I have been knitting non-stop for over five years now.

Knitting stuck. Perhaps it is because, to my constant and great surprise, I've finally found my people! I have been seeking this elusive feeling of fitting in for many years apparently in all the wrong places.

I am lucky and blessed to be among the community of knitters not just because they get me, but because I've learned so much about myself and the world in the process of bonding with a group of strong, talented individuals

My father passed away suddenly this April. The yarn and needles kept me from shrieking all the way down to Florida on the plane, which was a comfort to me and a relief to my fellow travelers. I repeated my knitter's chant in my head like a mantra — knit one, knit two, knit three, purl one — creating ribbing on a striped sock throughout the flight. It comforted and calmed me in ways nothing else could. It also spared the other passengers a slurpy, sobbing wreck on their flight. Lucky them!

Something akin to grace comes to me in my knitting. I am filled with elation when I realize that my rediscovery of knitting is, incredibly, opening my heart in so many ways!

Dawn Penny is biding her time as a professional secretary in Norfolk, VA while plotting her next career involving yarn. She is a recovering pastry chef who spends any spare time (when she's not knitting) fishing on the beaches of the Outer Banks, gardening, or entertaining her two cats and fiber-tolerant husband.

Drunk, Divorced,

& Covered in Cat Hair

Laurie Perry

Great love stories never begin with the phrase, *"I think we need to talk."*

The night I heard those six little words from my husband, I had cooked spaghetti for dinner. Now, I'm no Betty Crocker; I don't know baking soda from baking powder, and in my kitchen *everything* goes with red wine. Everything.

But spaghetti is a relatively confrontation-free dish, so I had a sneaking suspicion that he did not want to talk about pasta. Apparently I am psychic.

It was August – broiling hot outside, chilled to Arctic freshness inside. I sat cross-legged on the floor, flipping through a magazine, eating spaghetti at the coffee table. My husband sat across the room, flipping through channels on the TV.

"I think we need to talk."

And so began the conversation that ended my marriage. Before the month was out, he had moved into a bachelor apartment in a neighboring town; left me alone in our condo with four cats, an empty bed and hours of endless night.

I spent the next four months drunk, avoiding the word *Divorce*, and covered in cat hair. The very thought of me (me? *Divorced!?*) with four cats — well, it was so sexy and appealing that mere words could barely describe it. Most, if not all, involved some poetic combination of: crazy, cat, lady, spinster, eaten, dead, alone, alone, *ALONE*.

Thanksgiving came. Then Christmas, and New Year's Day, and I moved into a little house with all my cats and all my stuff, and fear and free time. There was a *lot* of free time, sleep had become a thing of the past. Goodbye, married life — farewell, slumber! So long, my true loves! Nice knowing ya'll!

Each night I went over the details of our demise, struggling to pinpoint the exact moment when the lines of communication had grown so twisted and tangled; when did the relationship become hopelessly knotted? After an hour of fitful sleep I'd wake, place one foot in front of the other, and stumble through the day blanketed with a fine layer of cat hair from knee to ankle.

Friends tried to entice me out of the house, but evenings it was just me, Patsy Cline and the cats. And ya'll ... you have never *seen* from the cat hair. THE CAT HAIR. If only I knew then what I know now — that you can spin fur into yarn — well, shit. I could have knitted a new husband.

But I'm getting ahead of myself.

Right after New Year's Day, my friend Shannon invited me to a knitting class. Knitting? Ah. Knitting – something maybe I could do on long nights with Patsy and our mutual friend, Jack Daniels. They wouldn't mind, we could knit together and remember the good ol' days. Knit sweaters without fear of a boyfriend curse – yes, knitting...

I could try that.

After a run-in with a lint roller I arrived at class to learn, in just one afternoon, the intricate magic of pulling a beautiful wood stick through yarn to make fabric. I saw fiber so gorgeous it was shocking, needles polished to a glassy sheen. And I learned to cast on, and to knit.

And it *took*.

I drove home with my new yarn and needles and I knitted. And I knitted. And DAMN YA'LL. I knitted. By Tuesday I was ready to join a new ball of yarn and I HAD NO IDEA HOW TO DO IT.

Did that stop me? Did the war of Northern aggression stop Scarlett? Oh *please*. I double-stranded and knit on. And on. My very first scarf was a testament to my determination. Right, wrong or indifferent, I would knit, dammit! Tomorrow?

After all, tomorrow is another day – for *knitting*.

Before long, knitting became my constant companion. I spent every evening with my projects, telling my

cashmere it was the George Clooney of yarns –
romantic, intimate, and a little beyond my reach. I
bought needles in all sizes and began to stockpile yarn
like it had been outlawed. I made promises I could keep
– promises of scarves and hats and one day (one day!)
a sweater. I knew this was real love because I eagerly
introduced it to all my friends, my family, my
coworkers. We were ON FIRE, me and knitting.

Sure, there were problems – there were issues. Every
relationship has its moments, its tangles.

But with this relationship, things were *different*. I could
just rip back down to the very core of the problems,
knit it all over again, purl where I should have known
better, love harder. Hold it tighter. Or not hold on so
tightly at all.

What I could have never known is that knitting would
inspire me to understand that not all mistakes are
flaws. I hear it at every Stitch 'n Bitch meeting, *"Those
aren't flaws! They're design elements!"*

I met other knitters, I got out of the house, my knitting
is covered in cat hair – but that's OK.

It's mohair anyway.

I've learned a lot from this relationship. Sometimes the
yarn runs out, or it's hard to find, or the extravagant
cost must be carefully considered. Yes – like all
worthwhile things – a fiber affair has it's price.

But you make do. You improvise. Life hands you plastic needles and crummy yarn, you get the wrong gauge, but you knit *through* it, and around it.

In spite of it all, I knit.

And *that* is a great love story.

Laurie Perry lives, blogs and knits in LA, where she writes about her adventures at www.crazyautnpurl.com.

Cabled Lives

Marta Kosh

I teach knitting. It is my privilege to teach new knitters in a small but very exciting yarn shop every Tuesday, in Southern Connecticut. As an instructor, patience is required not only for teaching new skills, but for listening empathetically to each student in my care. When I meet a new student there are several questions I ask as we choose yarn and begin working the knit and purl.

Did you knit in the past? Tell me who taught you? What was it like? What would you like to knit ? Who would you like to knit for?

Though these questions seem simple, they bring a wealth of life stories to the surface and can open hours of conversation. Each student who walks through our door has a tale to tell. They come to learn new skills, true, but just as often they come for knitting therapy. Many are courageous women who choose to take action with yarn and needles to cope with adversity, who refuse to view themselves solely as victims.

One skill they absorb with the knitting is what all knitters eventually develop, the ability to view aspects of their lives as parts of a knit fabric — to find analogies within their stitches to illuminate their own life journeys.

I love new knitters. The fiber world is opening up for them, and they can move in any direction they choose. I get excited when the knitted cast-on turns into the first knit stitch. it's an honor to share with my students the simplicity of the craft — only two stitches to learn! Two stitches which can combine to fashion a one-of-a-kind creation. My blessings come from new knitter's joy. Everyone thinks I am so patient, but who wouldn't stop and watch incredible birth!

Among the many beautiful students I have met, some stand out in my memory: The woman who wants to knit soft hats for her best friend who is battling cancer. A woman who knits by her terminally ill mother's bedside; another woman honors her mother's passing, refreshing her knitting skills as she recalls summers knitting on her family's Maine porch. Yet another daughter wants to finish and continue knitting Christmas stockings as her mother did.

But the most striking are the survivors; one student who wants to knit during chemotherapy; a woman with multiple sclerosis whose family cannot believe that she wants knitting lessons.

All of these students, whether they realize it or not, have discovered ways to use knitting and yarn to better understand and cope with their own life circumstances. I, myself, was a closet knitter who came out about three years ago when I read that a new yarn shop was opening in my town. I walked in the door of Janet Kemp Fine Yarns, and have never left. Not only am I a teacher, I am also an avid student.

Through encouragement, respect and love, the teacher-student relationship creates a circle of endless knitting possibilities. My own level of knitting has been raised. I am learning constantly from a staff who believes in my creativity, as I believe in the abilities and talents of my own new knitting students.

In the shop where I work we knit together often, and share every aspect of our lives. My own story is far from boring; a shipwreck of a childhood was salvaged by a complicated, but choice-filled adult life, rich with family and friends for which I am humbly grateful.

But as I work my yarn, teach my students and learn from those around me, I have come to realize that all of our lives are like knitted cables which twist, travel, divide, join and mutate as we move along on our life journey. And, in the end, isn't each cable full of complexity and beauty?

Marta Kosh lives in Connecticut on a small farm with her husband, Ray and their border collie, Simba. In addition to fiber arts, she teaches old world cider making at Boothe Farm. She uses her craft of knitting to connect with her fellow human beings and find balance in her life. Marta is also known as Marti and Luvknits to her family and many knitting friends.

Splicing & Plying

Minnie McKain

I have drawn solace and tranquility from fiber all my life. My paternal grandmother taught me to crochet when I was five years old. That Christmas I wrapped miles and miles of crocheted chains around our tree, thinking they made the prettiest garlands. My maternal grandmother taught me to knit when I was ten, and although I never learned to hold the yarn the way that she felt was right, I loved it. It was then that the hook and needle became a regular, steadying facet of my life.

Knitting, crocheting, and now spinning have long been soothing to me. The comments I hear now about knitting being the new yoga make me laugh, because I find yoga anything but relaxing.

I can remember crying over an afghan while I went through my teenage angst; hating boys, loathing school, and furious with my parents for being such dopes as to give me a curfew, of all things!

Crocheting was the only thing that kept the heartburn and heartache away during my first pregnancy. I was young and spent hours worrying about my baby, wondering if I was old enough to raise her.

Even though I've dealt with arthritis in my hands from an early age, I've worked through the worst times by knitting and crocheting.

Three years ago, my life fell apart. Within a month I lost my grandmother and my father suffered a severe stroke. As I sat in the waiting room with my mother, knitting to stay awake so that she wouldn't be alone when my brother checked with the doctor on my father's condition, we were both comforted by the rhythm of my stitches.

He never recovered, and 33 days after my grandmother's passing we lost my father, too. As my parents were both deaf, the task fell on me to interpret for mom through all of the funeral arrangements and family notifications. My hands ached, but my heart ached as well, so I returned to the haven of my sticks and string at the end of the day.

As so often happens in life, trouble followed trouble and later that year I found myself enmeshed in a nightmare when I discovered a terrible truth. My husband had been abusing my children while I was at work.

I was numb with guilt, pain and horror. When the numbness passed, I wept. I cried for three days. I couldn't eat, or sleep.

My oldest child told her stepmother, the abuse was reported to the police, and my other three children were taken from me. The county attorney's office determined — wrongly — that I had been aware of the situation and charged me with failure to protect my children. There is nothing more painful to a mother than the realization that she wasn't able to defend her children from such an malignant threat.

At the moment when I knew my children and I needed each other more than ever, we were separated, not permitted contact. The pain was overwhelming, wrenching, and laced with the knowledge that this had happened on my watch, in my home.

When the pain had finally subsided a bit, I turned once again to my fiber, this time with a purpose. Separated from my children, I decided to make them mittens and so that they could wrap themselves in my love. They weren't fancy; simple acrylic yarn in bright colors that most young children love. But I formed the stitches with love, longing and the pain of isolation. I have long hair which sometimes works its way into my projects — this time I left it in, sending my children a part of me.

I cried and crocheted on Christmas day, longing to hug, or at least talk, to my children. For 88 days I was not allowed to see my children, for 88 days I knit and crocheted.

Finally I was allowed to see my children, to hold and listen to them. Abuse rips families apart, the victims range far and wide. I've paid dearly for my inability to see and stop the abuse as it was happening, and may never be entirely reconciled with my oldest child. She has chosen a path I cannot follow, but it seems to make her happy, so I've worked hard to let that go. If the path decides to include me again, I will welcome her with open arms.

My other children are home now, and we are carving out a life for ourselves — a life in which we are all a bit sadder, and much wiser. My beautiful, independent second daughter lives with me as she attends college and reminds me of — well — me.

My older son grows more and more to look like his grandfather, whom I miss so much. My younger son has a mischievous grin, and beautiful blue eyes. I love them all, I am grateful to have them with me, I am hopeful that my daughter will return one day, and I knit.

Minnie McKain lives in the midwest with her fiance, daughter, two sons, and two cats. She has been knitting, crocheting, and spinning for those she loves, as well as for charity, for an accumulated time of sixty-six years, which is almost twice her real age. (No, she's not going to tell you that!)

A Shawl for Nana

Miriam Felton

Returning home from teaching a knitting class I found a troubling message from my mother on my answering machine. Her mother, my Nana, had been taken to the emergency room because of a heart murmur that finally had become too dangerous to ignore.

Nana knew about her heart problem, but it didn't seem very serious. When compared with the stomach cancer she had battled the previous year, it seemed downright insignificant.

However, Nana's diagnosis was not good. She would die if she didn't have surgery, but this same surgery might well prove too much for her heart (as it had for three of her relatives.)

I was shaken and weepy, I found that I couldn't concentrate very well. So I began knitting an alpaca lace wrap, which for me is a rather mindless project that doesn't require constant attention. Thankfully, working the lace took enough of my attention to keep worrisome thoughts at bay. The fingering-weight alpaca yarn running through my hands and over my slick metal needles, clicking rhythmically, helped calm my nerves.

When I began the wrap, I'd meant it to be for me. Memories of Nana, though, kept creeping into my mind, with every stitch I thought of her. I remembered her wonderful generosity, and how when any of us needed some blessing she would Storm the Heavens and launch a nationwide prayer campaign on our behalf, calling relatives all over the country to get them in on it. I remembered Nana's Portuguese Sweet Bread, the technique of which I spent a whole summer perfecting.

By the time I had ten repeats finished, I realized that the wrap would have to be for Nana. It might be the last thing I could make for her, and I wanted her to know how much she meant to me. What better way to show her that than through the countless hours and hundreds-of-thousands of stitches, each one formed with love and well-wishes.

Usually one thinks of grandmothers handing down beautiful heirloom knits to their grandchildren, and perhaps given a few more years, that wrap will become one. But I am content to know that Nana loves it, and someday, perhaps, she will return it me, reminding me of her when she is gone.

NOTE: At publication time Miriam's Nana is recovering and plans on enjoying her shawl for many years to come.

Miriam began handwork at a young age, learning to sew when she was 4 or 5 and following that up with crochet when she was 7. Miriam's designs and her daily ramblings about knitting, bookbinding, and life can be found at www.mimknits.blogspot.com.

Rebuttal

Elizabeth Rees

I take it here, I take it there,
I take my knitting everywhere.
In darkest wood when I'm out camping,
At the Doc's with belly cramping,
In rush hour traffic —lights permitting,
Sometimes walking, sometimes sitting.
I take it here, I take it there,
I take my knitting everywhere.

Knitting lace beside the fountain,
Socks while climbing up the mountain,
Purling down the winding roads,
On the creek-bank with the toads.
I take it here, I take it there,
I take my knitting everywhere.

I take it with me to my work
(Permit me one eccentric quirk)
Tuchas numb, in meetings mired,
Cabling keeps my thoughts inspired.
I take it here, I take it there,
I take my knitting everywhere.

I take it with me to the gym
Vain and strong and getting slim.
Aerobics, cycle, treadmill's cool,
Wrapped in rubber at the pool.
I take it here, I take it there,
I take my knitting everywhere.

I knit for love and charity
And sometimes even just for me.
On dark days when I cannot win,
It keeps me from the loony bin.
I take it here, I take it there,
I take my knitting everywhere.

The rhythm of the needles calms me
Unguent of Giliad balms me
Nicks and wounds? Undone with stitches!
Lanolin for nervous twitches.
I take it here, I take it there,
I take my knitting everywhere.

Husband enters, on cat feet creeping,
Quoth he, It's three! You should be sleeping!
He's right — good night! For now, I'm quitting,
But in Morpheus' arms, I'll still be knitting!
I take it here, I take it there,
I take my knitting everywhere.

Antisocial urges shriven,
Demons of my darkness driven.
If one day this peace disbands,
I've the weapons in my hands.
I take it here, I take it there,
I take my knitting everywhere.

*Elizabeth is a self-taught knitter — so she never learned what she couldn't do!
In Arizona's Salt River Valley she knits, writes, and designs for SouthWest
Trading Company.*

Desperately Seeking Distraction

Marie Harriman

41 year old female, *often in chronic pain, seeks non-medical diversion to enhance life and promote enjoyment.*

I am disabled and haven't worked for over two years, a victim of chronic migraines and Fibromyalgia, a disorder that causes muscle pain and fatigue.

I have qualified for the national dole and all of the high-powered pain medication modern medicine has to offer, yet those painkillers have drawbacks. In order to limit the physical and mental side effects, I prefer to postpone the use of these drugs until they are truly needed. A good distraction is priceless in bridging the gap between relatively pain free periods.

But I have a wonderful companion that provides an excellent diversion whenever I need it — Knitting.

Knitting occupies my mind for hours while the pain is at a low level, allowing me to function with minimal medication. A complex lace pattern requires so much concentration that I can forget about almost everything. Lost in knit-two-togethers and yarn-overs, I immerse myself in stitch marker placements while dreaming of how the final knit piece will look.

Hours pass blissfully, my mind is off my illness, my pain subsides — albeit temporarily. I have created a delightful oasis of peace and comfort in the middle of a pain-filled day.

Further, the knitting is good for my hands, arms and shoulders. I find myself stretching my arms, shoulders, and upper body to facilitate my knitting. This keeps my body less susceptible to pain, helping to work it out when it does occur. In other words, I work to keep in shape so I can knit!

During those fallow times when the pain has become severe and I'm confined to bed, my mind wanders to pattern design, mentally creating sweaters, shawls, shrugs and other knitwear.

I occupy my mind with vast catalogs of color, texture, yarn and garment silhouettes. Playing with these design elements in my head passes the time, distracting me from my pain. Eventually I drift off to sleep, comforted by the colors and textures I've dreamed up.

Knitting is my portable comrade, moving from the porch swing in Summer, to the couch in Winter, to my bed on more difficult days. Knitting waits with me in doctors offices and travels with me on trips with my husband.

My yarn doesn't hold grudges, allowing me to switch comfortably from a lace shawl to a pair of striped socks. My stitches don't mind if I split my focus between them and a good DVD, or even put the project away for a bit.

Knitting is an ever-giving companion that helps me through the discomfort and confusion in a difficult phase of my life.

Marie Harriman taught herself to knit during a year as an exchange student in Sweden, rediscovering her passion after disabling Fibromyalgia ended her engineering career. When not defending her yarn stash from her cats, she favors knitting sweaters and lacy shawls. She is currently repairing a pair of mittens her grandmother made over 50 years ago for her six-year-old niece. Upon discovering that relationships had a way of ending after she'd completed a sweater for the current boyfriend, Marie has no plans to knit a sweater for her husband (much to his dismay.)

Yarn Substitutions

Alice H. Boxer

I'm making an afghan, assembling granny squares.

At this point it's a methodical task. First the blocks
must be sewn into rows, then each long row sewn
together. It's reassuring work, work that my hands
know well. Each separate square, or block, has the
same number of stitches on each side.

The sides have to be lined up, stitches matched, before
they are joined together. The rows also must be lined
up, a similar process, only longer. The blocks are a riot
of color, almost garish. Each square is different. This is
by design.

Granny squares are a simple pattern, plain as dirt,
meant to use up scraps of yarn. They are made in
"rounds" even though they are square. The first round
has four lobes, like a flower or a shamrock. Each round
builds on the first, arithmetically.

The second round has eight clusters, the third twelve,
the fourth sixteen, and so forth. The classic granny has
four rounds, each round a different color, the last round
usually black.

The crocheter can match improbable colors fearlessly,
knowing that the black will tame things. The joining
yarn is also black, a thrifty, common color.

I usually like work like this, simple, soothing. I can put my brain in neutral and watch television or talk on the phone.

But this time, even though the task is uncomplicated, the work tugs at my memory, engaging me in complex and unexpected ways. When I made the blocks two years ago, I found myself with a surplus of half skeins and tag ends. I inherited them, some from my mother and the rest from my mother-in-law.

My mother's yarns; gold, coral, pink and a peppy green, were chosen with great care and came from her one project, an afghan. She made it during a period of enforced inactivity, recuperating from an operation. In a reversal of roles, I taught her how to crochet. I knew it was a skill she'd always wanted, so I was eager to teach her.

She sat patiently by my side as I showed her the intricacies of yarn and hook. I thought crocheting must have been a disappointment to her; she never made another thing. I felt I had failed her, failed to excite her interest in a craft that fulfilled me on many levels.

After she finished, she had no use for the yarn and gave it to me. Much later I discovered she suffered from Parkinson's disease. She hid it from her children for many years. Now I realize that I didn't fail her, her body failed her. But it makes me sad that she never drew the same satisfaction I did from crochet.

I never could teach my mother-in-law, Doris, anything. Our philosophies were diametrically opposed.

We couldn't agree on child rearing, bed making, cooking or religion. Often the only common ground that my mother-in-law and I had was crocheting. Every year she gave me a subscription to a needlework magazine. I've never actually made a single project from its pages, but I loved looking and imagining the possibilities.

Hands never still, her industry endowed her with virtue. Her output was prodigious; the yarns she left had more colors than my mother's, both brighter and duller. There were several different variegated yarns that had names like Varsity and Fiesta and — my favorite — Springtime.

When she went into a nursing home, I found this trove in a cardboard dresser, neatly stowed and sorted by color. These scraps were one thing I wanted for myself. I thought that maybe they would help me understand this difficult woman. What I found was that the gap between us was impossible to bridge completely.

So, I had the yarn, but not quite the time or inclination to do anything with all the tangled ends and knots. Sometimes I would go peek into the bag that held the yarns, marveling at the unexpected color combinations the twining ends would make. In the back of my mind was the question of just what I would do with it all.

That summer was a period of constant crisis. My mother-in-law was settled into a nursing home. My own mother was quite ill, requiring an operation. I could feel these women — women who had shaped my life — slipping away.

One day it came to me, a way to use those tangled tag ends of yarn; I could make granny squares. I could make some sense of those twisting, twining colors. So I began. Each block was to have some yarn from each contributor, a bit from Mom, a snippet from Doris.

Summer turned to Autumn and life became more difficult; out of the blue I needed an operation, too. The yarn went with me to the hospital. During my recovery, I sat and crocheted, round by round, tying myself to those other women.

Doris' yarn pressed me to greater creativity and experimentation with color. I began to feel less estranged from her sensibilities. My mother's yarn brought memories of our time together, drawing me closer to her.

I wove the bright with the dull, a fragment from one, a piece from the other. A rhythm emerged. Some of the blocks were all dark, but with a richness that the bright pastel blocks lacked. Some were dull, gray, beige, gold, with little spark. But they have their own quiescent beauty, a kind of promise, like a field of wheat stubble.

And now I'm finishing the afghan, putting blocks together, bright with dark, rich with dull, all bound in black. I have few insights into my mother-in-law's heart. My own mother took no pleasure in handwork and never crocheted another thing after she finished her one project.

But here spread out before me is the tangible product of all our efforts, an intersection of our lives. Maybe that will be enough to warm me in the years to come.

Alice learned to crochet sometime in the late sixties. Her first project was a long vest to wear with mini skirts! Although mini skirts are long in her past, crochet has been a part of her life ever since.

I Am Not Quiet

Amy Ripton

I am not quiet. I am not still. Anyone who thinks I have ever been either doesn't know me well. The four-year-old me decided that shy was no fun, and I haven't stopped making noise since.

Soon after my loud declaration, I was given my first needle, my first yarn, my first canvas on which to depict whatever the heck it was that I couldn't — or wouldn't — silence.

Understand — I am not always talking, though it feels that way sometimes. I am singing, tapping out rhythms, strumming away too. Often my body is making no audible noise. Then, the sound continues in my head. The soundtrack is so loud that it invades each of my dreams, which can themselves be deafening, but are often beautiful.

I suspect that if you cradled my head to your ear as if it were a conch shell, and listened close, you would hear not the sea, but a barn dance. And somehow I'd be singing, playing the tune, calling the dance, playing out the rhythms with my flickering feet, and having a conversation in some corner, all at the one time. This clatter and tune that is in my head is me, and I am not quiet. I am not still.

The needles saved my aunts, mother, grandmother, some of their sanity. They focused the chattering tot in a peaceful direction. Judy, the needle-giving aunt who fills so many of my best memories, taught me stitches because she saw how much I loved hers.

She taught me stitches because her beloved Grandmother had taught her stitches, and it only seemed right. She taught me stitches because she loved me. She taught me that a bad stitch was best removed and replaced by a better stitch — the kindest of cruelties one stitcher can teach another.

And she taught me that I could make anything I wanted to make, and that she would find it beautiful. She told the truth.

First, it was embroidery. I stitched flowers, animals, seas, letters, trees. The women in my family lauded my work, saying how like my Great-grandmother I was, and how her needles had crocheted enough lace to cover the mountains outside. My needlework let me converse with this great woman whom time had kept from me, and with the women she had known and the children she had fed and clothed and loved, who now did the same for me, thanks to her. These women were never quiet, and they were never still. I strove to be like them, and eventually I was.

From the embroidery, I took to larger, more practical stitching. I sewed costumes, skirts, dresses, curtains, coats. I clothed friends, counting the garments I had made for their beloved backs and fearing that I hadn't made enough. I saw they needed belts, and so I sought out weaving friends for lessons and soon wove belts. I saw they needed bags and hoods and so I learned to work with hides. I feared they were cold so I stitched all of my scraps together into quilts. I noticed they were quiet sometimes, so I wove them songs and knitted them stories, and in all of them some ghost of me appeared, needles in hand. The sounds in my head leaked out to them, and some of them called it beautiful. And I knew I was loved.

One needle wasn't enough, so I sought friends with two needles, and asked their help. My first attempts at knitting frustrated me; the needles cold and the yarn willful. I cursed and fretted over my failures, accustomed to easy skill. One friend carved needles out of antler, another friend gave them to me. The spell their kindness cast enchanted my hands into knitting.

I made scarves for my Aunts and Mother, to warm their honeyed throats. I made the wonkiest, saddest mistake of a hat, and a friend accepted it lovingly, still wears it proudly on her bright head. She is not quiet. She is not still. She is teaching me to spin, so I can knit the yarn we spin for our youngest new friends, many of whom were born to other women who make things because they want to make someone else feel warmth and love.

And many of whom make things because they must, because they are not quiet. They are not still.

You have pictured needle workers incorrectly. Conjure up an image of us from history — you imagine us quiet. We are not quiet. They were not quiet. They were not still. Arachne was cursed — or blessed even — with those spiders legs because she was not quiet. She crowed about the beauty of her work. And even after she was twisted into a small voiceless thing, she was not quiet. She wove away, and let her weaving do her yelling for her.

The Bayeaux Tapestry was stitched by loud women — this I guarantee — to depict the victories of men who failed to honor their mothers well enough. Betsy Ross was not quiet. She was a revolutionary. Suffragettes and labor organizers knitted and embroidered their protests while they were imprisoned.

Mother Jones, loudest of Grandmothers, was an accomplished seamstress. I imagine every stitch on every dress she ever made echoing with her booming voice. The women of Gee's Bend were loud, fast moving, and hard-working. They hadn't the luxury of stillness. Remember that when you stare at their work hanging in hushed galleries.

I will not be quiet or still until I am dead, and I finally know that my own internal clamor is a fine gift. I will lay my ideas and songs down on paper, I will chant out my words and sing out my tunes and hope the sound pleases someone else.

And I will stitch my thoughts and prayers into things I hope will last, so some other girl will see my work and know that her own loud head is good, and she will relish her own sweet noise.

Amy Elizabeth Ripton is a practicing fiber-artist, writer, and singer-songwriter and the Academic Director of the Potomac Celtic Festival. She is a daughter, sister, niece, aunt, friend, and wife who is daily reminded of her fortunate position in the best circle of kith and kin a girl could wish for.

Fiber Myopics

Holly Scalera

Fiber-myopics is not being afraid to live with every
fiber of your being.

It's the uncorrected threads
Threads of hair
Threads of wool
Threads of knitting poetry with metal,
and not being afraid
        to
    feck up and accidentally, become successful
    like I did when I "stumbled into"
    being a hair colorist on
        Madison Avenue, N . Y . C .
6 surgeries later
my upper respiratory system shot by all the chemicals
green ghost attacking immunity,
the very stuff of life
air...

Fiber-myopics is breathing
It's the earthy aroma of discovering felting with wool,
      and making my own floral-grown colors,
It's reinventing yourself when the burdens of the flesh
     become too remote
       to work anymore.

Fiber-myopics is realizing friends my age die,
     and they did, and so would I have
       if I continued hairdressing...
and that is how I found Wednesday nights
     were millinery class nights at Fashion Institute

of Technology
(and that saved my my "feeling sorry" for myself butt)

Fiber-myopics is making one-of-a kind pre K-MART
fabric
the ancients made
to
bury
their
queens
in.
Fiber-myopics is:
Rolling
Pressing
The water
The rolling, the pressing, the water.
The stories handed down in the
locks grown by women,
grown by camels, buffalos, goats, and lambs.
Animal fiber
        we keep cutting and reconnecting,
            reshaping the tones
till we leave, and it
gets
buried
back
into
the
ground
and back into the time…
Time and time
We change because
that's what life is
Fiber-myopics.

Holly is the author of <u>*Crazy Love Rides*</u> *and* <u>*Painting The House Pink*</u> *and is
the recipient of a 2005 Writer's Digest award.*

Finishing Lessons

Annie Modesitt

Every family has its own fabric made up of fibers of personality, circumstance and sentiment. Each member knits their individual strand into the material, sometimes too tightly, sometimes too loosely, leaving others to compensate in order to form an even tension.

The fabric of my family's life is made of strong fiber, replete with holes, knots, badly twisted stitches — as well as lovely colorful sections with deep hues and rich textures.

The family of my childhood was troubled. Severe financial difficulties, substance misuse and anger colored my youth with pain and guilt. I spent a good part of my adolescence loathing myself, my parents, my brother, our dog and any other witness to the ongoing abuse that passed as "normal" in our insulated world.

Living in an untenable situation, I became a teen runaway at fourteen — only to be returned home a month later to a house of turmoil and wrath. My next escape, this one sanctioned and permanent, was to college at the age of sixteen. My father had died a few months earlier.

His repeated threats that he would not permit either my brother or myself to become *"goddamned college kids"* were, at the end, hollow.

I was free, but I dragged my unholy, hole-filled quilt of shame and pain with me, blanketing myself when I craved the comfort of familiarity. It was the only respite I felt I deserved.

Important choices are seldom easy. A choice may *seem* obvious, but until one inhabits the skin of the decision maker, it's impossible to pass judgment. My parents made choices that were incomprehensible to me in my youth, but are now more understandable. Spinning the thread of my own life has made me skeptical of perfectionists, and more forgiving of the foibles of those whose decisions affected me so greatly.

In my professional life I've become adept at finishing knit garments — repairing mistakes and emphasizing beautiful areas. Any good knitter knows that the goal of finishing isn't to hide errors, but to understand how they happened so they can be fixed. Perhaps an accident is best approached by unknitting, dropping stitches back or even ripping out sections to rework it.

There are parallels between finishing techniques and the process one goes through to prepare for the end of a life, to mourn a passing while celebrating the miracle of existence. We learn from knitting not to become overly concerned when things seem wrong — we learn to knit on for a few rows and wait for the outcome.

Often a stitch pattern is not obvious until we have finished it, the last row of a repeat will tie all of the previous stitches together so that the motif is finally clear.

Thus it is with my relationship with my mother — now that the finality of death marks our intimacy I find myself able to see patterns that had been impossible to grasp while the stitches were still being formed.

We fear death. We dread the feeling of inadequacy that fills us when we realize we can't prevent the passing of a loved one — or ourselves. The finality of death overwhelms us to such an extent that a frank discussion of it is too upsetting for most of us. We speak in guarded, shadowy, cryptic code — our friends have gone ahead, crossed over, passed on. Perhaps in this haiku of departure we find a greater truth than we might if we relied on unambiguous words: death, dying, finished, ended, over.

Facing the end of a life doesn't have to be an entirely fearful experience. It can be an opportunity to ponder the work involved in making the "garment" of a life, a final chance to fix mistakes and resolve issues.

My last weeks with my mother, and my attempt to come to terms with her death, parallels my efforts to "finish" the knit garments I create every day. In both instances I look for uneven spots and repair them, I try to discover what went wrong, I weave in the loose ends. There were many loose ends surrounding my mother's death to tie up, to weave in — and to cut.

My mother was the source of many life lessons. Some I didn't realized I'd learned until I *retaught* them to myself, an echo of my mothers voice sounding in my memory.

A self-taught lesson sticks to the soul. I'm a self taught

knitter and finisher, cobbling together techniques from books, my own experience and from other knitters to create simple methods to complete garments.

As the end of my mother's life approached, I found consolation in my knitting, in my finishing. I became a self-taught mourner.

In an effort to move ahead in my life and find some point to the seemingly random losses of beloved family members and friends, I turn to knitting.

Not only am I calmed by the repetition of knitting, the meditation of the needles and yarn, but I find that knitting gives me a vocabulary to express my grief I haven't found anywhere else. Knitting has become more to me than a craft, it has become a method of self _expression and self discovery.

My language is the jargon of yarn, needles and knitting technique. When I use my knowledge of knitting to create analogies, I find that non-knitting enigmas become a bit clearer.

Each of us has the potential to build our own nonverbal language; the vernacular of a treasured craft, the ability to communicate with beloved animals in our lives, an aptitude for music or dance which allows us to expose strong feelings we might otherwise hide.

The use of color, touch, smell and sound to convey emotions that are too strong to be contained by words is a skill we all can develop.

Binding Off
The jarring, jolt that a goodbye is final — it comes at the oddest moments, and is a piercing slash each time it surfaces.

Blocking
Fitting a loss into reality — coming to really believe that a brother won't be at a graduation, that we can't call mom to ask advice. Perhaps it's more a case of redesigning reality to accommodate the empty space that has been left.

Joining
Drawing parallels between snatches of memory and current life — finding a way to patch the small pieces together to have something to seize and wrap ourselves in.

Weaving In Ends
Realizing that there is a time to put some memories aside, to find a conclusion for issues that need resolution — and to accept that some issues may never have the outcome we'd like.

Picking up stitches, creating the collar and button band
Grafting these memories into current life. Finding ways to include those who have passed in everyday conversation, allowing them to continue to figure in daily routines in important ways.

Closure
Coming to a place where memories can be shared with little pain. Achieving a realization that human life is finite, death is not a tragedy, a poorly lived life IS tragic.

Each passing will require a different type of closure, an individual way to explain the grief, a new myth for each soul that has passed.

I mourn, and I knit.

In blending these, I find peace.

Annie Modesitt is the author of <u>Confessions of a Knitting Heretic</u> & <u>Knitting Millinery</u> writes, knits and is a wife and mother in South Orange, NJ. She blogs about her designing life at www.modeknit.com/blog.

Nausea & Needles

(or never fly pregnant...)

Carie Morrison

I was five months pregnant with my third child when I boarded the first of many flights I would take over the next several days. My two boys and I were flying to Montreal, where I was leaving the Merry Men with my mom while I traveled with a friend through Scotland. Contemplating hours of uninterrupted reading on the flight to Scotland made me giddy with delight. With a third baby on the way and a new house purchase looming, this was to be my last big trip for a while.

We had traveled to Scotland several times, always with children, never with any problems. However, I had overlooked one tiny detail: I had never flown while pregnant. Each pregnancy is different — the level of motion sickness associated with this one was quite unexpected, and something I never care to experience again!

Let's just say I spent a lot of time cramming my pregnant belly and two small children — who would not remain alone in their seats — into the tiny bathroom. A learning experience! Children, this is how you spell, "Occupied." I was not the most popular traveler on either of our two flights that day.

Upon arrival in Montreal, my mom whisked us away in a vain attempt to discover some sort of miracle air-

and-morning-sickness-cure. I was scheduled on two more flights over the following two days — Scotland or Bust! How dumb am I?

In the midst of my in-flight suffering, the only fellow passenger who comforted me during the long, horrid hours of bonding with one air-sickness bag after another, was a woman who knit — a lot.

A kind Scottish woman and her husband, on their way home from holiday, got stuck next to the sick pregnant blonde who looked like death warmed over. I assumed that, like everyone else on each previous flight, they would try their best to ignore me and hope the flight ended quickly so that they could put as much distance between themselves and me as humanly possible.

Amazingly, this woman sat down next to me, said that I looked like I wasn't feeling well, and asked when the baby was due. Then she asked me if I knit. At the time, I didn't. She proceeded to show me, thereby literally changing my life.

Her project was the popular, portable sock. After four nausea-filled flights, all of my concentration was initially focused on simply remaining upright; but as she knit on, her hands smoothly fashioning row after row of what I now know is stockinette stitch, I forgot about the nausea.

For the first time in four days I wasn't completely engulfed in worry about the baby or obsessed with guilt for taking this trip in the first place.

My Scottish friends' hands were efficient, fluid; the repetitive motion calmed me. Watching the colors change as she worked held me rapt for the entire flight.

Almost three years (and yet another baby) later, I am a full-fledged knitter. Nothing soothes, calms, and challenges me like knitting. I have been delighted to discover a creative side of me that I had not realized I possessed. In the frenzy of raising four little boys, knitting provides fulfillment that I cannot fittingly describe. Taking the time for myself, even if it's only a few minutes a day, provides a balance that I had not previously been able to achieve — balance that is necessary to maintain a level of functional sanity.

All of the nausea was worth it, just to sit with the sympathetic Scottish woman and her sock.

Carie abides in domestic bliss in the Midwest with her husband and four boys. A self-professed geek turned stay-at-home mom, she yearned for something unique and new to entertain her brain; she found it in knitting. She is completely blindsided by the rewards of creating something with her own two hands; the same hands that wielded scalpels and test tubes, that wipe noses and wash dishes, can create beauty with sticks and string. It really is that simple.

Knittericks

Amy Polcyn

After a rough day at work
Putting up with a boss who's a jerk
How relaxing to sit,
Get the yarn out and knit
Non-knitters miss out on this perk!

Walking into the yarn shop I see
Fibers, colors encircling me
I stroll down the aisle
I can't hide my smile
A stunning, sublime place to be.

With two sticks and some string I can find
The means of relaxing my mind
With each knit and each purl
My tensions unfurl
A most perfect way to unwind.

Stressed out and unable to think
She thought that she needed a shrink
The fees were so high
Instead she would try
Knitting striped socks in blue, green, and pink.

Does your partner complain that your stash
Is eating too much precious cash?
If yes, be prepared
To tell them, Compared
To therapy — it's cheaper than trash!

Amy chronicles her knitting and designing progress at frottez.blogspot.com.

I Only Knit For My Grandchildren

Francine Marrs

This past year our family experienced a most wonderful and amazing Christmas. Recently my daughter and son-in-law had become foster parents to four children, siblings, whose mother had abandoned them. Secretly, I'd made three sweaters for the three youngest children in the weeks leading up to our first Christmas together.

I love knitting for family, and I have always told my grandchildren that I think of them as I knit. I tell them that each stitch says, *"I love you!"* However, I find it hard to fill all requests for sweaters and scarfs so I field most requests for knit garments by saying, *"I only knit for my Grandchildren..."* I hadn't realized it, but our new family of foster children assumed that this rule excluded them from receiving any hand knit gifts from me.

The youngest child, three years old, had been eyeing one of my projects for weeks but didn't have the courage to ask me for it. I wrapped it especially for her, and when she opened it, she hugged it and kept repeating, *"Mine, mine, MINE!"* The boy, nine years old, unwrapped his sweater, held it in the air and stared at it for a long, long time. I held my breath. He hugged the knitting tightly to his chest and leapt from the sofa into my chair, hugging me as hard as he could. I barely survived.

It was the reaction of the middle child, though, which touched me deeply. After losing custody and all access to his daughter, her natural father chose this year to compensate for seven years of neglect and missed holidays. He emptied the stores, dragging five or six garbage bags full of toys and clothing into the house for her.

Sitting on the floor, surrounded by every conceivable toy, book, puzzle, electronic novelty and enough clothing for six children, she opened my package. Inside was a sweater I had knit especially for her — I only knit for my Grandchildren!

Her shoulders began to tremble and shake as she buried her face in her hands. We were all concerned, not sure how to take her intense reaction. She began to sob and slowly crawled into my daughter's arms, who murmured, *"It's going to be okay, you're all right — we're all here with you."*

The little girl looked up into my daughter's eyes and said, *"No, you don't understand — Grandma loves me! She really loves me!"*

My daughter & her husband have begun the process to adopt all four children.

Francine Marrs is an adoption pioneer, having adopted 3 multiracial children as a single parent in 1971. She taught herself to knit at the age of 8 with yarn from a worn sock & toothpicks, and learns something new about knitting every month. Francine sells patterns which simplify knitting at www.knittingvault.com.

You Knit Like You Live

LeAnne Frank

I never used to think of myself as creative until I rediscovered knitting a few years ago. When I knit I can create something that will look good, make someone happy, and give myself a tremendous sense of accomplishment. But that's not really why I knit.

I knit because it's fun — pure and simple enjoyment at the end of a day. I can sit and knit and talk to my kids, enjoying the family time that just being together provides, a different kind of "warm and fuzzy". But I haven't always felt this way about knitting.

My mother tried to teach me to knit at age seven. One of my brothers gave me a ball of yarn and I began to knit a scarf. When I lost interest it became a doll's bed cover. (This must be genetic, as last year my daughter's first knitting project was not a scarf, as planned, but a bed cover for her doll!)

Between ages 10 and 17, I didn't knit at all. Of course, it wasn't cool and I was spending all my free time in the pool as a competitive swimmer. I returned to the needles, though, when I worked in New York City as a nanny between my freshman & sophomore years in college. The mother for whom I worked went to Ralph Lauren and bought a sweater for $465, asked her local yarn shop to create a similar pattern, knit the sweater herself and returned the very expensive original to the store.

She inspired me, and when she gave me yards of heathery blue wool I happily returned to knitting, working up one of the best projects I've completed. Alas, it looks a bit 1980s, with puffy sleeves and short, tight waist, but someday it will come back in style. Currently it keeps company with my grandmother's fur on the top shelf in my closet. During my nanny years I was also inspired to knit a Lopi sweater — a bit small now for me — which waits for my daughter to grow into it.

Knitting didn't figure in my life again I discovered that I was pregnant with my first child. I knit for the baby — booties, hats and even a sweater with a truck on it. The small projects fit tidily into the life of a mother of two small boys, but once I had my third child in 3 years, knitting fell by the wayside. Knitting may have helped me deal with the stresses of parenting three children under age four, and a marriage that was ending, but I felt unable to devote the time to my beloved craft.

Looking back, I wish I would have knitted then, it may have helped a lot. Hindsight is 20/20. I stayed away from knitting until one day when I met Alice at a soccer game. I have no idea how our conversation turned to knitting, but on that day I acquired a good friend. In our frequent knitting and chatting session, Alice and I have decided that how you knit is a good indication of life philosophy. Or, as Alice says, "You knit like you live your life."

For instance, I sometimes toy with the idea of not working up a gauge swatch at all for some projects, while another knitter may work up a swatch for a scarf!

Juggling a full time job with three children and a commitment to triathlon training makes for a very hectic schedule and I always seem to have many different knitting projects going on at the same time. Perhaps that's why it's such a joy to know that no matter which chair I plop into at home, there will always be a bit of knitting close at hand.

However, another knitter I know will finish one sweater completely, buttons and all, before moving on to the next project. This knitter has one knitting spot where she works when at home, and when she travels she carries all of her needles with her.

I admire her single-mindedness and organization, but it's just not the way I'm made. I love the fact that she always seems to be knitting a beautiful item for someone else, but I'm afraid I'm just much more selfish. I love making things for me! Alice is right: You knit like you live your life.

I try to fit knitting into every day and empty moment. I look forward to waiting the half hour for my boys to take their guitar and bass lessons; I anticipate a 3 hour drive to Seattle — as a passenger — as prime knitting time. I love going to the yarn store now (in past years it was a little like moving into the Grandma Realm) and I have nearly a dozen projects ongoing at any time:

There's the easy stockinette stitch whatever, perfect for working during conversation or a movie; there's the cable-while-increasing, detail oriented project that can only be worked with no TV or kids around; and just about every type of project in between! I don't even mind if my husband has to work until 8:00 pm, since it buys me an hour of knitting time!

Alice knitted through her divorce — at a time when she didn't feel very good about herself, she found in her knitting a tremendous source of self esteem. Embroiled in my third custody battle in eight years, I'm grateful for my knitting — I will need a lot of solace and calm in the coming months. I'm not instinctively a calm person. Knitting gives me peace, helps me set aside time with good friends, and provides a semblance of normalcy during trying times.

On Thursday afternoons Alice and I have started a knitting / playgroup for ourselves and our respective children — they love it! A group of eight-year-old girls play hide and seek while the adolescent boys retreat to the basement for video games.

When the older girls sometimes knit with the moms, we have to tone down our language. My 13-year-old son recently asked, *"When are we going to have knitting group again?"* which translates into, *"When's the next time I can have Doritos and Coke right before dinner as I play video games that you don't let me play at home?"*

I suppose we all have our own personal reasons for loving knitting!

LeAnne is a working mother of three fun children and wife to The Man-Who-Enters-No-Yarn-Stores. When not knitting she swims, bikes and runs the roads in her pursuit of her other hobby, triathlon.

Ode to 2 Sticks & A String

(with apologies to Elizabeth Barrett Browning)

Anne Marie Gunther

How do I love knitting?
  Let me count the ways.

I love knitting to the depth and breadth and
  height my fingers can reach
When feeling anxious for the click of
  needles and ideal bliss.

I love knitting to the level of every day's most
              quiet need, by sun and soft lamp light.
I love knitting freely, as I strive for perfection.
I love knitting purely, as a tool for meditation.
I love knitting with a passion and a trust.
I love knitting as a way to comfort lost dreams.
I love knitting with the anger, smiles,
  and tears of all my life.
And I love knitting best when instructing others.

Why do I teach knitting?
  To bring peace,
  creative energy,
  love of beautiful fibers,
  camaraderie,
  and the pure unselfishness of
  bettering the world through
  one stitch,
  one person,
  at a time.

Anne Marie Gunther is a Craft Yarn Council of America certified knitting teacher in the Philadelphia PA suburbs. When not teaching knitting, she knits for pleasure while she listens to baseball games or plays with her cats. She keeps a husband around just for laughs.

Creator

Evelyn Bourne-Gould

Knitting is a pastime and companion from childhood. I remember sitting at my mother's knee, the sound of her clicking needles bringing so much comfort. I remember the tears of frustration I shed as my mother and grandmother taught me to knit,"I'll NEVER get this!" But I did.

Now knitting has become second nature to me — I knit without thought, freeing my mind. I focusing inward as my fingers fly rhythmically, forming stitches, feeling yarn stream through my hands.

A few years ago I saw a flyer in my local yarn shop for a workshop,"Knitting as a Spiritual Practice." The group's facilitator, a counselor with art therapy experience, wanted to focus specifically on the craft of knitting contemplatively. We met in a comfortable living room space, sitting in a circle, listening to inspirational passages as we quietly knit.

Each person had the opportunity to share or just listen. During a period of silence a candle would be lit, and we would each pray quietly in our own way or simply meditate. Departing in peace, we would cling to the sacredness of time and space we had created.

My first exposure to the spiritual side of knitting, this

experience opened my mind and heart to the joy of contemplative knitting.

Life can often be crazy, hectic and stressful all at one time. In seeking to preserve my sanity and my connection with the Divine source, I have found that knitting has a calming effect. Knitting helps me find my center, focusing on the work of my hands allows the cares of the day to retreat. I am able to creates a space where I can simply be — returning to a place of oneness with my Creator.

While searching online for a shawl pattern, I discovered the prayer shawl ministry. I felt blessed as I read about this organization, which encourages people to make shawls using knitting or crochet to be given away to those grieving the death of a loved one or dealing with serious illness.

They are also given in celebration of the birth of a child, a wedding or an ordination. Working in small groups or alone, the crafters pray for the recipient as they work their love and devotion into every stitch of these shawls. The completed shawls are prayed over before being presented to the recipient. And thus a humble garment takes on a divine purpose, becoming a mantle of comfort — a wearable embrace filled with healing and love.

As I read the book, Knitting Into the Mystery, which tells the story of the prayer shawl ministry, a new path unfolded for me. I found a connection between my faith and my craft. Here was a way that an enjoyable hobby could be transformed into a ministry of healing and personal growth.

When I learned that my grandmother was not feeling well, I found some deep purple yarn and began my first prayer shawl for her. As I worked on the shawl, each stitch became a prayer. Knit 3, purl 3 became,"love, healing, peace," and "bless this moment." Like a soothing mantra I breathed these words as my fingers flew, an indescribable feeling of peace filled me.

I looked forward to my time working on the shawl as a sacred, meditative period when everything else seemed to melt away and I felt a tangible communion with the Divine.

I will never forget how thrilled my grandma was when I presented her with the shawl. She fairly beamed as I placed it over her shoulders, thin from the weight loss of illness. I explained that it was a prayer shawl, that I had been praying for her as I knit it. "It feels like I'm wearing a hug!" she sighed. Watching from across the table my grandpa asked,"Could I get a shawl, too?" I promised him that I would knit a prayer shawl for him as well.

As I was finishing grandma's shawl I found an online group, Healing Shawls, which proved to be a wonderfully diverse group of knitters who create prayer and healing shawls as a ministry. One member spun off from that group and formed another group called,

Prayer Shawl Swap, where members are paired up and knit a shawl for one another. Our preferences with regard to color, fiber or style of shawl are exchanged, and we also share prayer requests.

As we work on our partner's shawl, we pray and meditate over their concerns. It is gratifying to contemplate — and perhaps ease — the worries of a complete stranger as I knit for them.

Now I almost always have a prayer shawl on my needles. If I'm feeling stressed I pick up my work, form the stitches and pray for the recipient. Suddenly I am filled with peace — the process has come full circle. I am fortunate to have found a way to use my talents to bring joy, healing and encouragement to others.

I have come to understand that the process of creating a gift also provides renewal, healing and peace for the creator.

Evelyn Bourne-Gould learned to knit as a child and hasn't stopped since. These days she teaches and leads knitting groups knitting in Washington, DC, where she lives with her husband (who also knits a little) and their three daughters.

I Love Hue

Catherine Kittrell

My grandmother taught me to crochet when I was quite young, but I had never knitted until three years ago. I woke up one very cold and blowy Sunday in January with an almost physical itch in my hands.

I was compelled to drive to Michael's and pick out some yarn, needles and a "Look, Ma! I'm Knitting!" book. My first project was a garter stitch scarf in thick dark red chenille — not the easiest fiber to learn on — and for the first several inches the sides were awfully wavy. But I was in love with the feel of the knitted fabric, I was mesmerized by the color.

The scarf turned out far too wide, but by then I was obsessed.

I love the calming effect of forming stitch after stitch, I enjoy the creativity of fashioning something unique, I revel in the instant community I inhabit with other knitters; but what really keeps me coming back is the color.

It's no coincidence that knitting fever came in January. I live in the center of the Midwest, where Winters are long and cold and gray and cloudy — and endless. Many days go by when the sun makes no appearance, gray sky — gray snow — gray life. It's become rather fashionable for horticulturists to talk about the wonderful hues of the Winter garden; to spout about the muted shades of brown, gray and black; to point out that a truly sophisticated mind will appreciate the subtle winter palette.

My intellectual side understands their point. But after months of staring at a muddy gray sky, tired snow and bare brown branches, I want deep, rich reds and achingly clear blues. Fresh, bright, strong, deep greens, sunny yellows and soothing lavenders.

And that's what knitting does for me — it brings vibrant summer color and warmth into the middle of a dull and dark shivering cold winter. When I buy clothing for myself, I tend toward black and white — a nice neutral wardrobe. But when I choose yarn for knitting projects — invariably too much yarn for too many projects to tackle at one time — it's color that seduces me.

After that first scarf, I made burgundy wool mittens, flaming orange mittens, a crimson turtleneck and another chenille scarf — in a dusky blue this time. I created a lovely lavender cardigan that actually came close to fitting me quite well, sleeveless shells in soft pink and bluebird blue.

I knit a toddler's cardigan in a lovely variegated pink cotton and sweaters for new twin babies in different shades of the same yarn. I made a sage green cardigan for my mother's Christmas gift and a dark red homespun keyhole scarf and some more easy garter stitch scarves with showy novelty yarn — red and purple and blue faux fur and ladder yarns.

There were matching soft purple mohair sweaters for a four-year-old and her baby doll, and a lovely bright yellow cardi for her new baby sister.

More baby sweaters – one in a periwinkle blue, one in a fresh leaf green with a matching hat. My sisters-in-law received drop-stitch scarves made with a dark mohair enlivened by gorgeous flecks of red and orange and cream.

When I look back on these projects — some rousing successes, some decidedly not — what stays with me more than anything else, more than the texture of the yarn or the patterns or the stitches, are the colors; bright or muted, clear or heathered.

I go to work in the dark predawn Winter hours, coaxing a reluctant car to life in the frigid cold. I return home again under a murky sky, slipping on the black ice and dirty snow.

But all I have to do is go to my knitting bag or my stash armoire, and the color washes over me. I relax and breathe... I can almost feel the new softness of a Spring morning, feel the sultry heat of a July afternoon in my garden, smell the earthy tang of a Autumn evening by the river.

Wrapped in a shawl, I turn on the radio and pull out a current project, drinking in the glorious hues. In the dark Winter evening the whole world looks brighter.

Catherine Kittrell lives, gardens and knits in Iowa, where she is trying hard to keep her burgeoning yarn stash from taking over her small house. So far she has managed to resist the lure of spinning, but she fears it's a losing battle.

Lissy Friedman (copy editor / proof reader) is a public health attorney and freelance writer in Boston, MA. She has been knitting for only a short while, but already has gained wisdom, fellowship, and passion from her newfound skill. She founded a knitting group in her neighborhood, and spreads the gospel through her needles wherever she goes.

Printed in the USA by Fidlar/Doubleday

ISBN 0-9754219-8-0

ISBN 978-0-9754219-8-7 (13 digit)

Mode
Knit
Press